$$g_{24} = \not{\eta} \, 2 \, b_{,2}$$

$$\left(\frac{x_1}{\sqrt{b}}\right)_{,} = g_{34,22} + g_{34,11} \quad g_{4,}$$

$$\frac{1}{-5}\Big)$$

$$(g_{24,2} - g_{24,3})_{,33} = \sigma$$

$$(g_{34,1} - g_{14,3})_{,33} = \sigma$$

$$g_{14,1} + g_{24,2} + g_{34,3} = \sigma$$

Spezialfall $g_{i4} = \psi_{,i}$ $\quad \Delta \psi = \sigma$

Maxwell − Feld.

$$g_{14} = u_{2,3} - u_{3,2} \Big|_{-,3}$$
$$g_{24} = u_{3,1} - u_{1,3} \Big|_{-,3} \Big| _{1}^{-3}$$
$$g_{34} = u_{1,2} - u_{2,1} \Big|_{,2} \Big|$$

$$\left[u_{1,22} + u_{1,33} - (u_{3,3} + u_{2,2})_{,1} \right],$$

$$(\Delta u_1 - \text{div}(u_{i;i})_{,1})_{,33} = \sigma$$

$$\left[-\Delta u_2 + \text{div}(u_{i;i})_{,12} \right]_{,33} = \sigma$$

Es soll u_1 und u_2 geben, perkuliar. dann u

$$(\Delta u_1)_{,33} = \sigma \qquad u_1 = \frac{y}{r} = r_{,2}$$

$$(\Delta u_2)_{,33} = \sigma \qquad u_2 = \frac{y}{r} = -r_{,1}$$

$$g_{14} = u_{2,3} = -r_{,13} \Big| -\left(\frac{x_1}{r}\right)_{,3} \Big| + \frac{x_1}{r}$$

Who Was Albert Einstein?

Endpaper: Drawing by Albert Einstein—Einstein's last mistress, Johanna Fantova, next to his sailboat. To her right, Albert's head, and the words "Ich hab's" (I found it!).

Translation from the German to the French by Olivier Mannoni.
Translated from the French by Sharon Grevet.

© 2005 Assouline Publishing
601 West 26th Street, 18th floor
New York, NY 10001, USA
Tel.: 212 989-6810   Fax: 212 647-0005
www.assouline.com

ISBN: 2 84323 673 8

Color separation: Gravor (Switzerland)
Printed by RR Donnelley (United States).

GERO VON BOEHM

Who Was
Albert Einstein?

ASSOULINE

For Félix and Maximilian

Contents

A lone wolf, solitary and reflective. His requirements were few. To him, food and clothing were just the bare, dull necessities of daily life. He liked women, when they did not distract him. And he loved music, when it was by Bach or Mozart. Most of all, he enjoyed playing it himself—on the violin he nicknamed Lina—preferably in his tiled kitchen, where the acoustics were good. He was like his thoughts, captivatingly simple and infinitely complex. Absentminded, disheveled, sockless, with the eternal pipe in his mouth, he was "the professor" of our childhood imagination, as familiar as a fictional character. That is also why Einstein is the only scientist ever to become a pop art icon, on a par with Charlie Chaplin, Marilyn Monroe, and Elvis. A wise man who believed that wisdom is not a product of schooling but of the lifelong attempt to acquire it.

The article that Albert Einstein sent for publication to Annalen der Physik *on September 27, 1905, was only three pages long, but the formula it contained changed our perception of the world. $E = mc^2$ may be the cultural equivalent of Beethoven's symphonies or the novels of Thomas Mann, but* *the repercussions of that equation were infinitely more important. To the three known dimensions, Einstein added a fourth: time. Had it not been for him, we would probably still have no concept of the structure of space or the birth of the universe thirty billion years ago. Although Einstein was a confirmed pacifist, he laid the theoretical foundations that led to the manufacture of the atomic bomb. Later, in a letter to President Roosevelt, he provided the impetus for the Manhattan Project, which bought about the creation of the atomic bomb. For him, this was a way of changing the world. But what was his world and what did we know of him?*

"The most beautiful experience we can have is the mysterious. It is the fundamental emotion that stands at the cradle of true art and true science. Whoever does not know it and can no longer wonder, no longer marvel, is as good as dead, and his eyes are dimmed," he said. He, too, was ever shrouded in mystery. Our image of Einstein, the person, remains a contradiction. This man, who was perfectly capable of showing affection was, nevertheless, a terrible husband, who cheated on his wives. He loved children, yet he failed his own.

Prologue

He never saw his daughter, and one of his sons ended up in a psychiatric hospital. He was a traveler, yet he insisted on having an exact reproduction of his Berlin home built in the United States. The Jewish faith was an integral part of his identity, yet he loathed organized religion.

What made Albertl, as he was known in childhood, the man he was to become? What were the issues that stamped him most profoundly? What were his innermost feelings? What was the source of his intellectual power? Was the structure of his brain, which was removed from his skull after his death and is still studied today, exceptional? The chronicle of the nearly eight decades that he spent on this earth is the story, as fascinating as it is touching, of a flesh-and-blood man, who was just a bit different from the rest; the story of a life between the pinnacle of the mind and the depths of human nature.

Paris, January 2005

Albert and his sister, Maja, 1884.

1885

The trees had turned color along the Lindwurmstrasse in Munich. The falling leaves danced in the first strong winds of autumn. From time to time, the black-haired child with the big, dark eyes stopped to observe them as they whirled. He mumbled something to himself before continuing hurriedly on his way. Since October 1, every morning except Sunday, rucksack on his back, the 6-year-old left the family home on Rengerweg at precisely 7:35 and walked up Lindwurmstrasse to attend the Petersschule, a Catholic primary school located on Blumenstrasse, not far from the Sendling Gate. As he had previously taken private lessons, he was able to skip the preparatory course and enter elementary school directly. His fellow students included the elder brother of painter Franz Marc and the grandson of Wilhelm von Kaulbach, whose monumental painting *The Destruction of Jerusalem,* hangs in the Neue Pinakothek in Munich. He was a very good student, often at the head of his class in the ensuing years. He did his homework conscientiously and had a good rapport with his teachers. The only class he did not like was gym. From that time on, he had a profound dislike of physical education. This earned Albert the nickname of Biedermeier (Goody Goody). At home he enjoyed working on complex tinkering projects, building houses of cards to a height of twelve or fourteen stories, and fabricating delicate models with his Erector set. He would lose himself in his own world, often for hours, until he achieved the results he wanted. Results. Even then, whatever he did had to produce results. Otherwise, it was either boring or a waste of time. At a very young age, Einstein would enter what psychologists now call a flow experience (a mental state in which we are so absorbed by what we are doing that we lose all sense of time, and are imbued with intense satisfaction). In a flow state, whether you are a mountain climber or a physicist, a cook or a musician, you are at one with the object of your passion. Awareness is at its height. Optimally, the brain emits endorphins, happiness hormones that can be addictive. Very early on, Einstein was obsessed with flow. When he was in that state, it was practically impossible to speak to him. But his excellent, doting parents allowed him the freedom to take that distance from the world he seemed to need, and which remained for the rest of his life.

He would later refer to himself as an *Einspänner*, a German term that means a one-horse cart, but also refers to someone who prefers to be alone and is incapable of close relationships. Hermann and Pauline Einstein were quick to understand that their son could not be judged according to traditional criteria. For the first two years of Albert's life, they were worried by their child's hesitancy to make contact with the world around him. He did not speak, even in the most rudimentary way. He did not even try. His parents consulted several physicians. But then, shortly before his third birthday, the first words that came out of his mouth formed a complete sentence. "The milk is too hot" were apparently his first words. When his parents asked him why he had not spoken sooner, he responded, "Because before, everything was fine." Did Albert mistrust language as a means of expression until then? Was it an ambition to act like the adults he had attentively observed that induced him to speak in full sentences rather than use baby talk? Was it a desire to convey meaning through language—in other words, "pronunciation"—and not say something "stupid" just for the pleasure of speaking? It was undoubtedly more a matter of mistrusting the world of language: Terra incognita. Little Albert answered questions hesitantly, carefully forming the words with his lips after first "trying them out" softly. So he said everything twice, and the household employees referred to him as the "double-dunce." They were only partly joking. It was not until he was 7 that Albert lost that habit and began speaking completely normally.

Later, he would always insist that his thoughts were beyond words. "Words or language, as they are written or spoken, do not seem to play any role in my thought process... I do not doubt for an instant that our thought most often proceeds without signs (words), and that it does so, moreover, in a largely unconscious manner. Otherwise, how would it happen, sometimes, that we spontaneously 'wonder' at some event? That 'wonderment' seems to occur when an event conflicts with the conceptual world that is sufficiently ingrained within us." This "wonderment" at least partially explains Einstein's creativity. When he grew from childhood to adulthood, he retained a childlike sense of wonder. Harvard psychologist Howard Gardner studied the genius of Einstein and compared it to that of other giants of the mind. He concluded that when a revolutionary novelty occurs, childlike elements of perception and intellectual maturity meet like the famous fingers in Michelangelo's representation of Genesis. Likewise, Henri Matisse, who lived to a ripe old age and was bedridden when he took a new approach to his art, believed that we have no right to forget how to see the world through the eyes of a child. And Charles Baudelaire maintained that children were the "painters of the modern world." In reality Einstein never stopped being a child, in his limitless curiosity, his candor, and his freedom of thought. All his life, he had to be taken care of like a little boy, "because Einstein has no need that renders him dependent," his physician, Janos Plesch, wrote in 1949. "You have to care for him, because he would never ask for anything whatsoever. He has a fortunate disposition, prac-tically indifferent to circumstances and en-vironment, since it welcomes the most simple and the most complex with the same frame of mind. From that perspective, I could say that he is a man devoid of physical sensations. He is as insubordinate in his body as he is in his mind. He sleeps until he is awakened; he remains awake until you ask him to go and eat; he may go hungry until you feed him— and then eat until you urge him to stop."

At school, subjects like history, geography, and classical languages gave him plenty of trouble, but he always earned the highest marks in physics and mathematics. Greek was a nightmare for him, as was the mindless memorization required by his teachers. Later on, Einstein spoke of his "lack of memory for words and text." Both in grade school and in high school, he preferred to be punished rather than perform the "stupid ritual of rote learning." And punishment, at the time, was nearly always corporal. Physical pain dissipates quickly, thought Albert, while a useless burden on the brain has longer-term effects. He preferred to work out mathematical problems, particularly after getting his hands, at the age of 12, on his "sacred little geometry book," a scientific presentation of Euclid's *Elements*. In it, he found clarity, security, and... beauty. This was the period when the aesthetic criteria that would play a decisive role in Einstein's future research were formed. Until the end of his life, the beauty of a calculation and its resultant formula played a significant role in Einstein's desire to continue searching for the secret that unifies the world. The shorter a formula, the greater its aesthetic value. $E = mc^2$. Like a painting by Vermeer or Picasso, like a Bach fugue, a Beethoven symphony.

But several years would first have to pass, as Albert's personality took shape. The foundations had already been laid down. He had always had the ambition to "free himself from the chains of the merely personal," as he said, and from an existence "dominated by wishes, hopes, and primitive feelings." His grand objective was thus formulated. And little by little, he began to find an internal equilibrium, as if the security found in Euclid had also had an effect on young Albert's psyche. During this period, the tantrums that afflicted the weaker personalities around him also began, gradually, to subside. Such personalities as his younger sister, Maja, or the private tutor who was given the task of overseeing the preparation to enroll Albert in school when he reached the age of 5, a common practice in upper-middle-class families at the time. "One day, when something displeased him during a lesson, he grabbed a chair and used it to strike the woman tutor, who was so terrified that she ran off in fear, and never showed up again," wrote his sister, Maja, in her memoirs. In another fit of rage, Albert cracked Maja's skull with a toy shovel— years later, she did not remember exactly why he had done this. Clearly, she had bothered or contradicted him, and this had been the self-defense mechanism of a precocious putative recluse. Albert interacted with his peers only when it was unavoidable. Their wild games, their climbing sessions, and their jokes were foreign to him, a waste of time. Einstein must already subconsciously have had a singular relation with the phenomenon of time, a concept he would later revolutionize. What's more, he could, in a way, project himself beyond time. When he was thinking, time simply stood still. And Albert flew like a space capsule through the universe of his thoughts, and was not disturbed by all the events and noises that surrounded him. "Even in a noisy crowd, he was able to withdraw on the sofa...and immerse himself so deeply in a problem that the multitude of voices in conversation stimulated him more than they disturbed him," recalled Maja. Some scholars even believe that he may have suffered from a special sort of autism known as Asperger syndrome. This type of autism inhibits language development in childhood and causes social behavioral disorders, but does not create learning problems. On the contrary, such symptoms are found more frequently than average in the extremely gifted. However, those who are affected by it have a greater capacity for concentration, and their faculties of observation, coupled with an ability to engage in abstract thought, are particularly well developed.

The dance of the colorful autumn leaves in the wind as he walked to school in Munich, the oncoming winter—all this Albert took in attentively. Even in later years, at Princeton, he would still become enthused over the change of seasons and the arrival of Indian summer. He would don his lined cap and go out for a walk, but never a very long one. Perhaps his acute perception of nature inspired the ideas he expressed in an article published in 1929: "Everything is determined, the beginning as well as the end, by forces over which we have no control. It is determined for insects as well as for the stars. Human beings, vegetables, or cosmic dust, we all dance to a mysterious tune, intoned in the distance by an invisible piper."

We do not know if, when he was in school, he still believed in a God of creation or if he was already beginning to doubt. In 1927, Einstein declared, "I cannot conceive of a personal God who would directly influence the actions of individuals, or would directly sit in judgment on creatures of his own creation... My religiosity consists in a humble admiration of the infinitely superior spirit that reveals itself in the little that we, with our weak and transitory understanding, can comprehend of reality."

Albert was the only Jew in his primary school class, and he attended Catholic religious education classes. The teacher took an immediate liking to this inquisitive, interested boy. Their respect was mutual, until one day when the teacher harshly made him understand that he was merely being tolerated among his Christian classmates. That day, the religion instructor brought a long nail to class and declared that the Jews had used such an implement to nail Jesus to the cross. This stirred up anti-Semitism already latent at that time, as Einstein later recalled. "It was based on racial characteristics of which the children were curiously aware and on impressions from religious teachings. Physical attacks and insults on the way home from school were frequent, but in most cases not too cruel. But they were sufficient to consolidate even in a child an acute feeling of being an outsider." So he was doubly an outsider in the world. But that was part of Einstein's identity, on a par with his mane or that famous photo where he stuck out his tongue at the photographers.

At school, he accommodated to an authority that, in reality, he rejected with his entire being. In the German Empire, schooling also comprised military drills and required total obedience. Discipline and order were paramount. "The teachers at the elementary school appeared to me like drill sergeants, and the teachers at the *Gymnasium* (high school) like lieutenants." It is hard to imagine a harsher judgment. He also detested the parades where the students had to line up along the edge of the street and wave their flags. The uniforms frightened him as much as the goose-stepping. Albert felt collective discipline was worthless. "When I grow up," he told his parents, "I don't want to be one of those poor people."

His parents accepted this attitude. They preferred to encourage their son's interests, his love of mathematics and, soon, for music as well. Pauline Einstein, his warm-hearted and affectionate—but stubborn and somewhat possessive—mother, had an intense passion for music. This was perhaps her way of compensating, in a household where there was so much talk of technology and business. She was a remarkable pianist, and she dreamed of some day playing music with her son. He was barely 6 when she started taking him for violin lessons. Pauline was always present at those lessons, as much to encourage her son as to head off any tantrums. But there was nothing for it: Albert went through several instructors with no audible results. The études and technical exercises bored him profoundly. Once again, drills proved counterproductive. However, at age 13, he fell in love with Mozart's sonatas and became determined to play them. The ice was broken. "Mozart's music was so pure and perfect, that one felt he had merely found it—that it had always existed as part of the inner beauty of the Universe, waiting to be revealed... My wish to reproduce them [the sonatas] to some degree in their artistic content and their unparalleled grace forced me to improve my technique; this I acquired with those sonatas, without ever practicing systematically. I believe altogether that love is a better master than duty—at least for me," Einstein later said. Despite his love of music, he never became a virtuoso, but some who heard him play claim they never heard music played "with greater fervor or more profound sensitivity." His physician, Janos Plesch, himself a great music lover, observed him at chamber music recitals in Berlin in the 1920s. "He has plump, somewhat elongated hands, with long, pointy fingers, totally different from the bony fingers of a Richard Wagner or a Franz Liszt. The delicacy of those fingers allows Einstein to achieve a clear tone almost instantaneously. What he lacks is a high-level technique, and poise in his bow technique in particular. He knows this. This inadequacy aggravates him, particularly in difficult passages. In such moments of anger, this man who knows no envy is nevertheless overcome with fits of jealousy." His beloved violin, Lina, provided rest for a mind wearied with reflection. Music is a vehicle that allows to continue thinking, and Einstein made use of it. Results. Everything had to have results. "I start by improvising; if that doesn't work, I seek consolation in Mozart. Yet, if I find an opening when I improvise, I need the brilliant constructions of Bach to prolong my reflections." Einstein especially liked to play in his kitchen, where the resonance was good.

The year Einstein was born in Ulm, 1879, was not an ordinary year. Thomas Alva Edison had invented the incandescent lightbulb, triggering a revolution. His displays of electric lights, which attracted hundreds of thousands of spectators, were the fires announcing a new era. That same year, in Berlin, the first electric tramway went into service. Alexander Graham Bell's telephone had already been in operation for three years. In 1885, Einstein's father, Hermann, and his brother, Jakob, founded the electrical-engineering factory J. Einstein & Cie. in Munich, rightly thinking that the opportunities were greater there than in Ulm. Jakob had worked in the town as an engineer, and Hermann had had some success as a featherbed merchant there. In 1885 the two brothers spent their first profits on the purchase of a house, and their wives shared the cooking. The families lived together in harmony in the house, and there was rarely a dispute. However, there were animated discussions every evening around the dinner table. Uncle Jakob guided Albert in his first scientific and theoretical reflections.

Naturally, they discussed the new adventure of technology, examined its prospects, and explored possibilities and solutions. This was not a bad environment for little Albert. His home comprised a laboratory, a workshop, and a boutique. The young boy saw how dynamos and telephone systems were manufactured; the business held seven patents. Observation and small manual tasks further spurred Albert's interest in technology and the secrets behind it. He could not yet guess that one day he would work in the Bern Patent Office and again question reality. In the meantime, his father and his uncle were developing the electric lighting network for the village of Schwabing; in 1886 they installed the first electric lighting for the Oktoberfest in Munich. They were the Edisons of the Bavarian capital. Albert Einstein's interest in the relationship between science and technology, and the phenomena that derived from them, also took root in that environment. He was especially enthralled with the popular science books of Aaron Bernstein. His reading also included Alexander von Humboldt's classic, *The Cosmos: A Sketch of a Physical Description of the Universe*, and a few works by Charles Darwin. Then, one day when he was 5 years old and sick in bed with a fever, Albert had his first encounter with a natural phenomenon. He would have liked to play with his Erector set, but he was not allowed to get up. Every hour, his mother changed his compresses—which he hated—and praised him for his patience. When Albert's father came home from work that evening, he had a present for his son: a small compass. Fascinated by the behavior of the needle, he immediately began to wonder about the origin of the phenomenon. Sixty years later, he wrote, "The fact that the needle behaved in such a definite manner did not fit at all into the pattern of occurrences that had established itself in my subconscious conceptual world—effects being connected with 'contact.' I can still remember—at least I believe I can remember—the deep and lasting impression this experience made on me. There had to be something behind the objects, something that was hidden." He believed that this episode had been a sort of spark, and looked for an explanation in later years. "A person has little insight into what takes place within himself. Seeing a compass for the first time may not produce a similar effect on a puppy, nor indeed on many a child. What then is it that determines the particular reaction of an individual? More or less plausible theories may be constructed about it, but one does not arrive at an in-depth understanding."

The mystery remains. Not everything can be explained. Period. Even subsequently, he always accepted this. Einstein's biographer, Albrecht Fölsing, sums this up in one perceptive sentence: "We will have to content ourselves with the suggestion that a productive result probably depends both on the 'wonder' and on the person 'wondering'."

In 1888, Albert entered the Luitpold Gymnasium, a renowned institution. There, too, he found the drills and the teachers obtuse, but he accepted some of them. His troubled relationship with words and language also improved during this period. Dr. Ruess, his history and German teacher, succeeded in communicating to Albert his enthusiasm for Schiller, Shakespeare, and Goethe. These authors were not unfamiliar to Albert, as sometimes, after dinner, his father read to the gathered family. Having adapted an old European Jewish tradition, the Einsteins welcomed into their home a guest "in need" every Thursday. When Albert was 10, Max Talmud, a penniless medical student, started coming once a week to lunch with the Einsteins. Max understood the intellectual hunger of the family's eldest son, and regularly informed him of the latest scientific breakthroughs. He recommended authors to Albert and discussed mathematical and philosophical problems with him. And he encouraged him to read Immanuel Kant's *Critique of Pure Reason*.

Albert immediately understood that Kant had once pursued the same objective as he: certainty and purity of thought. The three questions that Kant wanted to answer preoccupied Albert all his life: What can I know? What ought I to do? What may I hope for? These somewhat strange reflections on space and time by the philosopher from Königsberg (1724–1804) intensified Einstein's precocious interest in the subject. The Kantian concept that God may not exist stayed with Albert from that point on.

During the years at the Luitpold Gymnasium, where Jewish religious instruction was provided, the Prophets and their wisdom naturally began to impress Einstein. He also studied the preacher Solomon. He took the ritual requirements of Judaism seriously, although they were not particularly practiced in his freethinking household. He composed hymns to the glory of God and sang them aloud while walking home from school. The books he read in the following years would, however, turn Einstein's religious fervor into a passionate freethinking. It was also during this period that he "actually realized the vanity of the hope and quest that drives most people restlessly through life. ... Everyone was condemned, by the existence of his stomach, to participate in this race. Taking part in it undoubtedly satisfies the stomach, but not the man, as a thinking, and sentient, being. There the first way out is religion." He quickly found another way out, one that allowed him to leave school. Exactly ten years would pass before he began building his revolutionary intellectual structures.

Albert Einstein in 1898.

1895

The summer of 1895 was particularly hot in northern Italy. In 16-year-old Albert's small room at Via Foscolo 11, in Pavia, there was not a breath of air as he launched into his first scientific writing with a feverishness that was almost maniacal. He had fled Munich at the end of the previous year—to escape not only his authoritarian teachers but also the narrow German mind-set, the loathsome atmosphere that already oppressed him so greatly at the time, and that he would despise until the end of his days. Hermann and Pauline Einstein had left for Italy on an impulse, accompanied by Albert's sister, Maja, and Uncle Jakob's family. After its initial success, their electrical engineering company went under in 1893. The brothers had bet everything they had on a single hand, in an attempt to win the contract for lighting the Munich city center, and lost. Their competition had been two major industrial groups,

Siemens and Schuckert, and the latter had won the contract; anti-Semitic sentiments had apparently played a role in the decision. The company's sudden collapse and the reasons for its failure, which were certainly discussed within the family, frustrated Albert and presumably justified "his very distant attitude toward his native land, even prior to 1933," in the words of his biographer, Fölsing.

Albert's parents had left him in Munich to complete his secondary education. But they had not considered their son's rugged independence— although he had been asserting it for quite some time—and strong will. Who would have thought he would leave the gymnasium shortly before graduating? The last straw was a sharp dispute with his homeroom teacher. Albert always sat at the back of the classroom, ostensibly to show how bored he was. His absent look and sardonic smile were a provocation. For months the teacher ignored him, and then he lost patience. He criticized his student's impossible behavior and poor grades, crying, "Einstein, you will never amount to anything!" Then, the principal, whom Albert liked quite well, gave him a warning and asked him not to return to the gymnasium. In any event, Albert had only one thought in mind, and that was to escape. To leave the "lieutenants," the drills, the lessons learned by rote, which diverted him from true knowledge. Furthermore, he was alone in Munich. This was not the deliberate, elective solitude of the *Einspänner*, the one-horse cart. He missed his family, his mother, his Uncle Jakob and their technology outings. And he missed the long family dinners and chamber music with his mother and Maja. Neither then nor later in life did Albert have the character of a stoic whom nothing could touch. He was not one of those legendary scholars with a Buddha-like composure. His emotions seethed within him, but he knew how to hide them well. In 1917 he wrote in a letter, "I have discovered the power of mutation inherent in all human relations, and I have learned to protect myself from heat and cold, such that a temperature balance is practically ensured." But this pertained solely to his external temperature. The brother of family friend Max Talmud was a physician. He wrote Albert a medical certificate saying he was suffering from "neurasthenic exhaustion," and recommended a temporary leave from the gymnasium. Albert also asked his mathematics teacher for a certificate stating that he had achieved sufficient mastery in that subject to graduate, and that he was the best in his class. Then he headed for the central train station in Munich. This was in December. Several hours later, the train entered the Saint Gotthard Pass to Milan. Everything went dark. The book Albert was reading fell from his lap. On the other side was Italy, a new world. He would later speak of the following summer as the "happy months of my time in Italy," and said "his best memories were those anxiety-free, careless days and weeks."

He spent much of his time exploring the region and its inhabitants. Italy made a strong impression on Albert. The country appealed to his powers of observation and his sensuality. Its beauty, the mindset of its people, and their language all combined to give him deep satisfaction. Everything seemed better to him there than in his native, rigid, and dull Germany, which he had already permanently broken with, in spirit, by that time. It was not simply a matter of nostalgia for Italy, however, but a more complex sentiment.

He talked about it nearly forty years later. "When I crossed the Alps into Italy, I was very surprised by the language of the average Italian, whose words expressed profound thoughts and genuine education, in contrast to the average German. This reflects the long history of the culture. The people of northern Italy are the most civilized I have ever encountered." He quickly learned the language and very much liked its sonority, which delighted his musical sensibility. In the end, he experienced a veritable rebirth. He spent his first months in Italy with his parents on Via Berchet in Milan. The city fascinated him. He spent hours walking its streets, looking, listening, smelling, and touching all the things that had so delighted Friar Bonvesin de la Riva in the thirteenth century, which the latter had referred to as "the miracle of Milan." He traced the footsteps of the Enlightenment, which had embraced Milan more than any other city, as would the Romanticists after them. Then, the family moved to Pavia, which he disparaged: "The soul of this city can be roughly expressed in mathematical terms: (1) as the sum of the *Ladstöcke* that these ladies and gentlemen have devoured, and (2) as the impression that the uniformly dirty walls and streets give the visitor. The only good thing about it is the graceful, adorable little children."

One thing that was certain was that his parents were horrified when their son, their eldest child, the most gifted, announced to them that he was dropping out of school.

His father, who was fighting for his financial survival and trying to make a fresh start, took this opportunity to try to convince Albert to become an electrical engineer. Then his son could take his place in the company and one day run the small factory that the Einstein brothers had opened on the bank of the Naviglio di Pavia. That was his father's dream. The son reacted to this family pressure in his own way: he abruptly told his bemused parents that he wanted to become a professor of philosophy and specialize in the works of Kant. It is doubtful that Albert was serious, but at the time he was something of a provocateur. He actually had bigger plans. He was feeling an increasing need to be productive, and perhaps to question the way in which the world was physically represented. He pulled the ace from his sleeve: the letter of recommendation and the excellent reports from his previous high school in Munich. Although he was two years younger than the minimum required age, he wanted to use them to gain admission to the famous Polytechnikum, the Swiss Federal Institute of Technology in Zurich, and had studied on his own to take the entrance examination. He canvassed manuals and physics treatises with a maniacal attention to detail, in order to acquire a broader general education.

Finally, to prove that he was an independent thinker, einstein wrote his very first scientific essay entitled *Examination of the State of Ether in the Magnetic Field*. In the rare moments when he was not studying, he helped out with the family business. Uncle Jakob and his assistants came to ask his advice when they needed mathematical solutions to their technical problems. Problems they were unable to solve in several hours Albert worked out in just a few minutes. "This boy has a great future," said his uncle. But for the time being, the young man had failed the entrance examination for the Polytechnikum. He was not yet 17. He owed his failure to French, biology, and chemistry, subjects that did not interest him and where his education had left gaps. But this may have actually been a good thing; the following year was one that would have a profound effect on him, particularly from a human standpoint. He went to Aarau—the capital of the eponymous canton, located about thirty miles from Zurich—and finally worked on earning his high school diploma, which allowed him to avoid imminent conscription to military duty. The very idea of being drafted filled him with horror. The cantonal high school Albert attended was considered a liberal and top-notch one. There he completed his high school education in an entirely different atmosphere. And he came to understand natural authority in an environment diametrically opposed to the one he experienced at the Luitpold Gymnasium in Munich, with its military structure. The period he spent in Aarau had an effect that lasted his entire life. "With its liberal spirit, the earnestness and serious-mindedness of the instructors who were accountable to no outside authority, that institution left an unforgettable impression on me; the comparison with the six years I spent in a German high school run with an iron fist made me truly understand just how superior is an education based on freedom of choice and self-accountability over an education that relies on regimentation, external authority, and ambition. Real democracy is not an illusion," he wrote forty years later. Although his Greek and history instructor Jost Winteler taught in another division of the institution, the teacher's family took Albert in as a boarder. Their estate, Rössligut, became a second

Der Erziehungsrat

des
Kantons Aargau

urkundet hiemit:

Herr **Albert Einstein** von Ulm,

geboren den 14. März 1879,

besuchte die aargauische Kantonsschule & zwar die **III. & IV.** Klasse der Gewerbeschule.

Nach abgelegter schriftl. & mündl. Maturitätsprüfung am 18., 19. & 21. September, sowie am 30. September 1896, erhielt derselbe folgende Noten:

1. Deutsche Sprache und Litteratur _____ 5
2. Französische " " " _____ 3
3. Englische " " " _____ —
4. Italienische " " " _____ 5
5. Geschichte _____ 6
6. Geographie _____ 4
7. Algebra _____ 6
8. Geometrie [Planimetrie, Trigonometrie, Stereometrie & analytische Geometrie] _____ 6
9. Darstellende Geometrie _____ 6
10. Physik _____ 6
11. Chemie _____ 5
12. Naturgeschichte _____ 5
* 13. Im Kunstzeichnen _____ 4
* 14. Im technischen Zeichnen _____ 4
* Hier gelten die Jahresleistungen

Gestützt hierauf wird demselben das Zeugnis *der Reife* erteilt.

Aarau den 3ten Oktober 1896.

Im Namen des Erziehungsrates,
Der Präsident:

Der Sekretär:

Einstein's graduation diploma, 1896.

home to the aspiring scientist, a surrogate for the family home he had just lost once more. Pauline and Jost Winteler, who themselves had seven children, soon became "Mama" (he affectionately called her "Mamerl," or little mother) and "Papa" to him. His discussions with them, over leisurely dinners, also left an impression on him. The topics ranged from science to culture and, especially, politics, to which Papa Winteler introduced him "in a literally visionary manner," as he later acknowledged. Although "Papa" sometimes seemed a bit bumptious, "a prophetic spirit," he was already—in the late-nineteenth century—warning against the rise of German nationalism. He knew whereof he spoke. Winteler had studied in Jena and had observed the rise of nationalist feeling, especially after the Franco-Prussian War of 1870–1871. The atmosphere that reigned in paramilitary organizations and noble circles, caught up in the spirit of militarism, spoke volumes to him. The rationality of the Swiss point of view, with its republican traditions, confirmed Einstein's desire to distance himself from his native country. Freedom of thought was what he was after. His father, Hermann Einstein, never talked politics. Now

Albert had a companion with whom he could discuss such topics.

His interest in nature was another thing he had in common with the Wintelers. On weekends they took long hikes in the mountains. They identified plants, observed rare birds, and listened to them sing. On occasion Albert would disappear from the group at the same time as Marie, the 18-year-old daughter of his host family. Finally alone with her, even if for only a few minutes, his pulse would race.

When Marie was around him, he felt a strange tingling and a lightheartedness he had never experienced before. She was able to tear him away from his books; they often played piano duets together. A superintendent from the Ministry of Education noted at the time that during a recital, the student Einstein's violin playing excelled in its "sensitive interpretation of an adagio from Beethoven's sonata." No wonder. When he played, he was thinking of Marie. When she was out of sight, Albert missed her in a way he had never felt before. No doubt about it: Albert was head over heels for the first time.

When he wrote to the girl he adored—only one of these letters, sent while on vacation at his parents' home in Pavia, has survived—his tone was sweet and emphatic.

"Thank you, thank you so much, precious, for your affectionate letter, which gave me boundless happiness. It is so wonderful to be able to hug to my heart this small piece of paper that was lovingly gazed upon by two such dear eyes and prettily handled by such graceful hands. My angel, I now understand the meaning of the words *homesickness* and *longing*. But love causes far more happiness than longing does pain. Now I realize how essential my dear little sunshine has become to my well-being." And Marie spoke of her desire "to caress that forehead exhausted with study." She felt over-whelmed by "an acute understanding of [her] dearly beloved curly head" and "dear, great philosopher." But Einstein was not looking for an intellectual partner in Marie. His perception of women was gradually beginning to take shape. He would even sometimes call this girl two years his senior "my dear child." In the meantime, he left for Zurich to pursue his studies. Although he sent his girlfriend his dirty laundry to wash, by this time other "creatures" had taken her place: the "uncompromising angels" of science. Now he needed as little distraction as possible. The feeling that Marie could no longer get along without him—and he without her—worried him. And worry was not a feeling that he needed just then. He had to put some distance between them. Characteristically, he did not send his breakup letter to Marie directly, but to her mother. Authors Roger Highfield and Paul Carter had this to say about it: "The power of Einstein's letters to Pauline Winteler indicate that the feelings he confessed to her were as intense as those he felt for her daughter." They demonstrated this by quoting from his letter of May 1897, in which he also described his return to a world that he had already mastered as a child, one that would subsequently play a decisive role in his life. It was a reflection of his existence, his universe, in which he would always be the central figure. Other people could be nothing more than intruders if they wanted something from him. Einstein was well aware of the hurt he could cause those who tried to get close to him.

"It fills me with a strange satisfaction that I am now tasting some of the pain that my impulsiveness and my ignorance of such a tender soul have caused the dear girl. Relentless intellectual work and observation of God's nature are the inexorably uncompromising angels that will guide me through the twists and turns of this life, inspiring me with sweet sentiments, and giving me greater strength. If only I were able to give some to that good child! Yet this is a strange way to weather life's storms. In moments of clarity, I see myself as an ostrich, the bird that buries its head in the desert sand so as not to perceive danger. Thus we create our own little world, as pitifully insignificant as it may be, in order to deal with the perpetually changing dimensions of the true Being. Yet like a mole that has dug its own hole, we still feel a strange greatness and importance. Why would we demean ourselves? Others will see to that. So let us stop there."

It is as if he wanted to start by proving to himself what he was capable of achieving; afraid of being sidetracked from a grand objective, the price of love seemed too high to him. Depend on another human being or allow another to depend on him? Depend on feelings? Unthinkable! He had long been an addict, but his drug of choice was thought. He was now 19 years old. Marie Winteler had been a teacher in Olsberg for quite some time. Albert no longer wrote to her, and she would never again find happiness. Her marriage with the manager of a watch factory ended with a divorce in 1927. Robert Schulmann, an Einstein scholar, had access to Marie's personal documents from the years following her breakup with Einstein. During that period, she spent a lot of time away from work due to illness. Albert's granddaughter, Evelyn Einstein, even speculated that Marie's ill-fated relationship with the young scientist had thrown her into "mental confusion," and that she frequently underwent one of the treatments that were in common practice at the time. She spent the last years of her life in a rest home. Einstein's friendly relations with "Mamerl" and "Papa" Winteler were not affected by this more or less tacit separation. Sometimes, on weekends, Albert returned from Zurich to Aarau just to see Jost Winteler, and to exchange ideas with him and Pauline on current political events, flora and fauna, and music. Later, even though he had not married into the family, he was very pleased to have a family connection with the Wintelers. Albert's sister, Maja, married Marie's brother, Paul; and his best friend, Michele Besso, married Marie's elder sister, Anna.

It was in Zurich, while playing music, that Einstein had made the acquaintance of Besso, six years his senior, a mechanical engineer with a strong interest in physics. This dynamic but slightly chaotic man, his face adorned with a full beard, his head crowned with a dense, frizzy mane, came from a cosmopolitan background. He was the son of a Jewish family living in Italy. They had their roots in Spain and could trace their history back to the twelfth century. All of that pleased Einstein. Michele became and remained his best friend for life. Both men died in 1955, Besso one month before Einstein. In 1896, when Michele gave Einstein Ernst Mach's works on physics—which had an immediate and important influence on his development—while carrying on an ongoing philosophical dialogue with him, Einstein had already entered the Polytechnikum. There he was finally allowed to pursue his education, and did so with fervor. He was soon singled out by the professors, and he singled out one of his classmates.

No one has ever understood why Albert, a handsome and very charismatic man, became interested in Mileva Maric, a dark-eyed Serbian girl from Austria-Hungary, with a sensual mouth, four years his senior. She was somewhat humorless where he was concerned, and had a slight limp as a result of tuberculosis, which she contracted as a child, leaving her with a deformity of the left hip. Later, when asked whether that bothered him, and why he would consider marrying a girl like her, he answered, "Why not? She has a beautiful voice." Both were outsiders to the close-knit society of Swiss students—the Serbian girl and the now countryless young man who had arrived from Germany via Italy. When he applied for Swiss citizenship in 1899, he was asked questions that supremely irritated him, such as "Do you lead a respectable life?" and "Did any of your grandparents have syphilis?" The Swiss authorities had him investigated by a detective, who concluded that Einstein was an extremely ambitious, hardworking, and particularly stable young man, who also happened to be a member of the Temperance League. He had passed the first hurdle. In 1901 he became a Swiss citizen. Mileva, then nearly 21 years of age and the only woman in Department VI at the Polytechnikum, seemed dreamy and withdrawn in group discussions. Her rare remarks were laconic and sharp. When she was alone with Albert, she blossomed and revealed an enthusiasm that she showed to no one else. Ideas erupted like sparks.

Without a doubt, Einstein was in love with her mind. They visibly formed an ideal team, Albert with his practically limitless imagination and capacity for abstraction, and Mileva, a pragmatist endowed with logic. Einstein made increasing use of the young woman's abilities. She devoted much of her time to him, and if she failed a crucial exam, it was undoubtedly because she no longer had time to work on her own studies. She began to sacrifice herself.

Einstein's intelligence required him to use other people as sounding boards. Marcel Grossmann, with whom he studied mathematics, was one of them, as was Michele Besso. But since he never stopped thinking, even during the evening and at night, Mileva's presence suited him to perfection, especially when it came to thinking about relativity. He had long dreamed of combining energy and matter into a single formula—the eternal dream of a formula that would explain the world. It was Mileva who ventured the farthest into that space that Albert held sacrosanct, his thoughts. She was the first one to whom he talked about them in detail. And she helped him with his calculations. However, her contribution to the birth of Einstein's revolutionary theory and formula has never really been established. "My mother," wrote Mileva's son, "helped him solve mathematical problems, but no one could assist him with his creative work, with the constant stream of new ideas." Yet, in 1901, he wrote to the young woman, "How proud and happy I will be when together we have successfully completed our work on relative motion!" Physical attraction had been combined with intellectual attraction for quite some time; the couple had been having sexual relations for two years. Mileva, a woman of principle, had fended off his advances for a long time. She had thrown herself into her studies because a girl in poor health was considered "unmarriageable" in her cultural environment. She even left Zurich and Albert for a time, and went to find refuge at the University of Heidelberg, in Germany. A pregnancy would have jeopardized not only her career, but also her reputation. In Serbia she would have been considered a *kurva*, a whore, however, she eventually forgot her scruples, and gave in to her beloved's urging. From that moment on, sexuality played an important role in Einstein's life. It was an escape valve that briefly put him back in touch with the body that he neglected the rest of the time. But perhaps he did still think about his formulas when he was in bed with Mileva, and saw numbers when in the throes of passion. He would soon say, even to Mileva, that he felt aroused when he read a good physics treatise. In any event, sexual activity was a stimulation he would never give up at any price. "How beautiful it was, the last time I was able to hold your little body, just as nature made it, next to mine," he wrote after a lovers tryst at Lake Como. And Mileva also awaited Albert's next visit impatiently: "Until then, I'm going to work very hard in order to be entirely free to spend time with you. Little god, how beautiful the world will be once I'm your little woman. You'll see, there will be no little woman in the world happier than I, and the little man will surely be happy as well." She was soon pregnant. The fears that had been dissipated by the giddiness of love were soon borne out. Roger Highfield and Paul Carter analyzed Mileva's state of mind: "For her, a young woman who increasingly viewed herself as a victim and who was capable of dealing with obstacles only when she was feeling optimistic, the news had to be devastating. She was alone, far from her family, and just two months away from retaking the examination that was so important to her self-confidence and career aspirations. Her lover was a destitute dreamer who did not have marriage plans in his immediate future, whose parents rejected her, and who did not yet have a job." The happiness she dreamed of moved even a little farther out of reach. She was proud to be carrying the child of the man she so admired, but in May 1901, shortly after receiving the news, Einstein wrote her a letter from Winterthur, where he was working as a locum tenens at the Technical College, while Mileva remained in Zurich. In his opening lines, far from expressing joy at the prospect of fatherhood, he spoke about...sciences!

"My dear little Mileva! I just read a marvelous treatise by Lenard on the production of cathode rays by ultraviolet light. This fine study filled me with such happiness and pleasure that I feel compelled to share them with you. Be brave, my dear, and don't worry yourself sick. I won't leave you, and I'll see to it that everything turns out well. Just be patient! You'll see, you'll rest easily in my arms, even if things are starting out a bit awkwardly. How are you doing, my dear? What is the little one doing? Imagine how wonderful our life will be when we can once again create together, without being troubled, and no one can say a word to us! All of that dazzling pleasure will erase your current worries, and the days will slip by calmly and peacefully."

Mileva failed her exam for the second time. She just could not concentrate on it. In November, she returned to Novi Sad, Hungary, where her parents lived. There Mileva gave birth to a girl, most likely in late January 1902. Einstein never saw her, and would probably have preferred to erase the child from his life. Even his closest friends knew nothing of the birth of his daughter. He considered her a burden and an obstacle to his career with the Bern Patent Office, where he would soon start working. He was right about that. In Switzerland, public servants had to be model citizens. And his parents continued to put strong pressure on him. They absolutely refused to give him permission to marry Mileva, and, in fact, he did not marry her until after his father died in October 1902.

Not much is known about their daughter, whom they named Lieserl, and what became of her. According to the in-depth research undertaken by New York author Michele Zackheim, the child died of scarlet fever at the age of twenty-one months, after possibly suffering a mental handicap brought on by the disease. That may have been another reason why Mileva wanted to keep Lieserl away from Einstein, who would not have tolerated her. Mileva returned to Switzerland without their daughter. Mileva's parents probably took care of Lieserl, from the time Mileva left Novi Sad until the little girl died. Did Einstein force Mileva to give the child up for adoption? In any event, the attraction he held for Mileva seems to have been more powerful than the young woman's maternal instincts. But the "uncompromising angels" of science prevailed again. Although Einstein inquired about Lieserl's health just after she was born—"Is she healthy? Does she cry like she should? What color are her little eyes? Which one of us does she favor? Who feeds her her little milk?"—immediately afterward, he became intrigued with birth as a biological phenomenon. "One day, I, too, would like to make a Lieserl; I imagine it is very interesting."

Mileva must write to Albert about the little girl, photograph her or draw her, but she must never be brought into contact with him. In truth, the trip between Switzerland and Novi Sad would not have been a problem for him; it was barely a day away. He just did not want to make it. This was when his relationship with Mileva fundamentally changed. In the early 1960s, his eldest son (born in 1904), then unaware of the existence of a sister, said, "Something happened between them, but Mileva told me that it was 'extremely personal.' Whatever it was, it preoccupied her, and Albert was apparently responsible for it. Mileva's friends advised her to get it off her chest; it would relieve her. But she maintained that it was too personal, and she kept it to herself her entire life." This dark secret, this drama that, in all likelihood, they never spoke of, even between themselves, had a devastating effect. While they did marry, in reality Einstein was already severing his ties with Mileva, at least mentally. So why did he marry her? Was it because he knew that she had long been dependent on him, and this was his way of dealing with such an inconvenience? Was it because, when all was said and done, he was a good-hearted boy, or because he needed her as a scientific sounding board, a partner for intellectual discussions? Or was it because her sexual temperament suited him?

In any event, Mileva would soon follow him to Bern, where Albert had found work at the Patent Office. On June 23, 1902, he started work as a provisionally elected "Technical Expert III Class." It was a routine job, but one that interested him, since it involved patenting all sorts of devices for the electrical industry, from typewriters to tools used for daily household use. It left him enough time to develop his theories and to think about his own inventions. The tinkerer was in his element. Later he would file his own patent applications for a noiseless refrigerator and a new apparatus to aid the deaf.

But for the time being, just after leaving the office, he would delve ever deeper into the mysteries of space and time. His goal was within striking distance.

Einstein at the Bern Patent Office, 1905—the year
he published his theory of relativity.

⌒⊙

1905

"An extraordinary, supernatural power must have been concentrated in that body. Nothing, truly nothing, could have diverted him from that single direction that his existence was taking and for which the entire eternal flame, the entire greatness of his soul, everything about it that was alive, seem to be saved up and waiting there," wrote Max Brod about... Johannes Kepler, the main character in his novel *The Redemption of Tycho Brahe*. But he was really talking about Albert Einstein, whom Brod had met at the home of Bertha Fanta, an influential intellectual who hosted a salon in Prague. A friend of Kafka's, Max Brod observed the young Einstein more acutely than anyone else. Admittedly, he could not have known him very well, but the psychological portrait that he depicted in the character of Kepler was perfectly accurate. "In Tycho's eyes, the calmness with which he went about his work, totally disregarding appeals by flatterers, had something superhuman about it, an indescribable insensitivity proceeding from a distant, frozen region... He was reminded of that popular tale where a soldier of fortune sold his heart to the devil in exchange for some bulletproof armor. That was Kepler. He was heartless. And it was precisely for that reason that there was nothing in the world that he feared. He was incapable of love. And, consequently, he had a natural confidence when it came to sentimental problems." Brod's book was published in 1915, four years after the author observed Einstein in Prague. At the time, Einstein was already world famous. The year 1905 was his annus mirabilis—that miracle year when he produced three papers that would forever change the world.

The most important of these was entitled *On the Electrodynamics of Moving Bodies*. It was received by *Annalen der Physik* on June 30, and on September 26, it was published. Einstein got practically no sleep early that year. At night he worked on the thoughts and formulas that would later go down in history as the theory of relativity. He meticulously polished each and every word. Mileva was always at his side. Later he would say, "I would rather live and work in a lighthouse, so little do I depend on others from a scientific standpoint. I don't need them."

In reality, he very much needed them. In his day-to-day life, for example, if others did not take care of him, he forgot to eat, and starved. And when he was doing his scientific work, he needed others as sounding boards. Later his colleagues spoke of how important feedback was to him in gauging his thoughts. When he was giving a monologue, he needed listeners. That year his primary listener was still Mileva. She was his support in his nightly battle to construct his theory. She would begin by listening to him patiently, and then ask him questions—the right questions.

Gerald Holton, a professor who studied the origins of the theory of relativity, said, "From the start, they always read books together. Einstein was a man who needed books and he needed someone to talk to. There is no doubt that they talked a great deal about his work."

Mileva was the one who would go in search of the documents Einstein needed for his research. And it was she who verified his data. The master needed only give her a key word, and she would take off on her search and quickly and meticulously do her calculations. "It's my wife who takes care of my mathematics," said Einstein. She could not help him with the creative side of the theory of relativity. No one could. He had already had the concept in his head for ten years. Indeed, it had been developing since Einstein's great intellectual experimentation in 1896: back then, he had wondered what would happen if you were to run after a ray of light. Now he had to give logical and mathematical shape to the problem. It took Einstein five weeks, during which he exerted himself. At first he was relaxed. Visitors recall seeing him rocking the cradle of his son, Hans Albert, then 1 year old, with one hand, and writing his formulas with the other. When the baby cried, he sang something to him, but continued writing. Einstein later described this creative process, recalling those moments he spent with his son.

"We were like a little child upon entering a gigantic library, whose shelves are filled from floor to ceiling with books written in the widest variety of languages. The child knows that someone must have written those books, but he does not know whom, and he does not understand the languages in which they are written. The child then notices that the books are arranged in a certain order, a mysterious sequence, whose principle he does not know and can just barely guess." Einstein was the eternal child in the library of the universe. His objective: to find the book written by "the Old One," as he called God, the operating instructions for everything. Einstein perceived the formula, glimmering behind a veil. Deciphering it cost him every bit of energy he possessed. Being a genius was exhausting work; he was incapable of that easygoing manner we often attribute to highly gifted people. Finally, his body went on strike. Once the manuscript was posted, he spent two weeks in bed while Mileva nursed him. It was done. In his paper, Einstein challenged Isaac Newton's vision of the universe, a vision that had prevailed for two centuries: Newton considered space a finite physical reality through which the stars and planets traveled in measurable motion.

He also believed that time was an invariable and absolute flow, coursing through an immutable past toward an infinite future, and that God directed everything, as it were, from an imaginary control room. This had long disturbed Einstein, the thinker, the skeptic, the amateur philosopher. It had taken ten years for his thoughts to ripen from the time he had read Aaron Bernstein and his popular science series. He recalled this, visualizing the dog-eared pages before him, remembering the Gothic print. "Space, time, and light are closely related," wrote Bernstein. Since it takes time for light to travel through space, the image that we see is only a reflection of the past. "In that sense, what we see is never the present," asserted Bernstein, thereby triggering fireworks of thought in young Albert's brain. It takes eight minutes for the light of the sun to reach the Earth. If the sun were suddenly extinguished, it would take only eight minutes for darkness to fall upon our planet. If the sun were a gigantic clock with an illuminated dial, it would be eight minutes ahead of our own watches. In 1905, Einstein applied his intuition and mathematical skills to the issue of correcting and expanding upon these suppositions "inspired" by Newton. He discussed and he calculated. He talked with his friend Michele Besso and worked on mathematics with Mileva. His model was a cosmos in which the stars, planets, and galaxies moved in relation to one another and not in relation to a closed space created by God, in which there is an objectively fixed point. If that were the case, an observer standing at that point would have the impression of being the only stationary object in the universe, with everything else in motion around him. On the contrary, Einstein believed that no one is entitled to special privileges.

Everyone is equal. Why should this not likewise apply to the universe? This notion was not based on scientific reasoning, but on the thoughts of a man who, early on, almost mysteriously became a humanist. In the final analysis, the theory of relativity stems from the sense of wonder that he retained from his childhood. At the age of 16, he was already asking himself the question, what would it be like to travel with a light wave at a speed of 186,000 miles per second, to ride it, to run after it? Is light then motionless? Does it descend into darkness? These questions pursued him even in his dreams. He wanted to provide the definitive answer. This was not simply a matter of a physicist's curiosity; Einstein was well aware that he was bordering on the ultimate mystery. The shape of the Creator glimmered behind the veil, like the formula itself. Einstein was convinced that the world operated according to the same laws for all observers—even for those fortunate (or unfortunate?) enough to ride the light. In the cosmos, no one is entitled to special privileges. The principle of equality was firmly anchored in his mind, and not with respect to physics alone. All of the philosophers who interested him had challenged codified structures, preached tolerance, reflected upon freedom of thought, and influenced the Age of Enlightenment. Kant, Spinoza, and finally, Hume, with his positivist philosophy based on critique and rationalism, were early influences on Einstein's thought processes. What's more, this also accounts for his love of humanity as a whole, like the unity he strove to achieve in his formulas. On the other hand, he had trouble feeling affection for individuals. From that point of view, he was always the skeptic. He was a reclusive philanthropist, whose philanthropy held as long as everyone kept to a distance.

Later Einstein referred to Hume, "whose treatise on understanding I studied shortly before finding relativity theory. Without those philosophical studies, I might not have arrived at that solution." But what was that solution?

A stroke of genius prompted him to reconcile two elements: the principle of observational equality and the constancy of the speed of light. To the three known dimensions, Einstein added a fourth: time. This was developed later on in the general theory of relativity. In one fell swoop, Einstein showed that time can be warped and that the universe is curved. A revolution in physics was achieved. If his intellectual work was so innovative, it was because it occurred at a time when theoretical sciences were not yet recognized in their own right. The experiments conducted at the institutions of the day were not particularly exciting. It was not a period when scientists tried to get to the bottom of things. The industrial revolution was still in full swing, and research scientists were primarily concerned with what they could add to the pot: steel, dyes, railroads, fertilizers.

Then this young scientist arrived on the scene and, at the ripe old age of 26, turned our perception of the world on its ear. The scientific establishment's reaction to this loner was reserved. Even many experienced physicists could not understand him. The core of Einstein's theory entirely refuted the prevailing concept of time. Einstein predicted that a watch in motion necessarily ticks more slowly than a motionless watch. Temporal distortion was a threat to what was then believed to be "reality." People believed they could assign an objective date to time, a single, simultaneous "now" for the whole world. But the theory of relativity precisely showed that simultaneity is only relative and defined in the context of our own reference system. There is no such thing as objective simultaneity.

By the time his paper was published, the editor of the *Annalen der Physik* had already received an addendum from Bern. In it, Einstein unveiled the truly sensational element of his theory. That brief addendum dealt with the relationship between mass and energy. It showed that the mass of a body decreases in proportion to the energy it releases in the form of radiation. Consequently, all energy has mass. The true meaning of that addendum would not be revealed until two years later, when Einstein demonstrated that the converse was also true: all mass has energy. The equation $E=mc^2$, which he used to describe this relationship (E being energy, m mass, and c the speed of light), is the most famous formula ever written. If c is 299,792,458 meters per second, c^2 is a gigantic number. This means that an enormous quantity of energy can be derived from a miniscule mass. Theoretically, an original energy is lying dormant in every stone, in every plant. But it is especially from fissionable material that enormous quantities of energy can be extracted, for example, from the mass lost when the nuclei of heavy atoms, such as plutonium and uranium, are broken down. That is one of the main conclusions of the theory of relativity. Forty years later, the atomic bomb confirmed this in a dramatic way. From a scientific standpoint, Einstein did not take part in its production, but he did write a letter to President Franklin

Roosevelt, encouraging work on the project. He regretted it after the first atomic bomb was dropped on Hiroshima, in 1945. But that was still four decades in the future.

Little did he know that—along with the quantum theory he developed later on—he had created the theoretical basis for progress that, over the course of the twentieth century, would entirely change our world: computer chips, networking, biotechnology, and a new cosmology. These interwoven innovations have something in common: they speed things up, and, in an ironic twist of fate, they cause us to perceive time in a way that is entirely different from the way it was perceived in Einstein's day. The world seems to be turning faster. Was that his intent? Just before his death, he experienced the era of acceleration, but he was no longer around to see the effects of the revolution he started. He did not see the radical way in which scientific progress is now achieved. It has been a very long time since scientific truth has relied on the wisdom of the past. "In what way is today's computer scientist still concerned with Newton? A thin layer of recent knowledge is sufficient for him to practice his art. Scientific progress is so radical that, at every stage, it is able to throw away almost all the baggage of its own history," wrote science historian Brian Appleyard. Have the sciences have become the religion of our time? Sometimes, the only things that seem to count are the results research scientists expose for adoration like a holy grail. Have culture and history been sacrificed on the altar of science?

Einstein himself was proud of his global culture. In 1905, the Einsteins were intoxicated with triumph. That year, Einstein apparently told Mileva's father, "Everything I have created and achieved, I owe to Mileva. She is my brilliant inspiration, the guardian angel who preserves me from the sins of existence and, even more, from those of science. Without her, I would never have begun my work, and I would not have completed it either."

Einstein never clearly specified the origins of his theory of relativity. His paper published in the *Annalen der Physik* contains no bibliographic information, something extremely unusual for a scientific publication. It was later said that Mileva had brought a decisive experiment to his attention, and in 1921, Einstein himself would say that it was his first step toward the theory of relativity. The so-called Michelson-Morley experiment, conducted in 1887, examined the speed of light to determine whether it

Albert Einstein and Mileva with their eldest son, 1907.

was influenced by the relative motion of the ether (the element that was thought to carry light waves). It found that the speed of light was identical, regardless of the circumstances. But we will probably never truly know who or what provided the decisive inspiration for the theory of relativity. Einstein himself could not have cared less. The only thing that concerned him was the results he achieved. He now thought of himself as unassailable. What was it that Tycho Brahe said about Kepler in Max Brod's novel? "You have regard for nothing. You go straight down your sacred path… In reality, it's not the truth that you serve. You serve only yourself, your purity, and your virginity."

Later, in Prague, Einstein would become aware of his increasing isolation from the day-to-day world. From his office at the German University, he could see the garden of the neighboring lunatic asylum and compare himself with the people confined there. "There you see some of the madmen who aren't working on quantum theory."

In 1911, after an interlude in Zurich, the family went to live in the golden city of Prague. There, Hans Albert attended school, made progress in his piano lessons, and "joyfully asked his papa interesting questions about physics, mathematics, and nature," Mileva wrote to a friend. The boy was a good deal like his father. After school he often sat on the banks of the river and observed the speed of the water flowing through the sluice gate. He would later become a hydraulic engineer. He clearly had the gift of projecting his thoughts into the workings of energy sources—as his father did with the cosmos. Or perhaps he was just looking for an excuse to return home as late as possible, since he could feel the tension mounting between his parents. The Einstein marriage was on the rocks. With fame came mounting social obligations, and Mileva was mistrustful toward other people. Although her intellect was practically on a par with Albert's, she had become more housewife than scientific assistant. Furthermore, she had to run the household with a firm hand, in order to continue to have some role to play. Hans Albert would later say that, after his eighth birthday in 1912, disputes between his parents became more and more frequent. Einstein became increasingly acerbic, and Mileva gradually withdrew. Hatred settled in. Hans Albert took his mother's side. Einstein accused Mileva of setting the children against him and progressively distanced himself from the family.

He had met his cousin, Elsa, again in the spring of 1912, and they began an intimate relationship that would last seven years. He later divorced Mileva and married Elsa. Mileva had done her duty as a scientific assistant and wife. Unlike Einstein, she would continue to care for the children. From that moment on, Einstein would only want a wife capable of making a home for him, while tolerating an occasional extramarital affair. Elsa took care of Einstein, did the housework, made him his "bird food," as he called it, and soup to nurse his increasingly ailing stomach.

1915

Albert and Mileva had separated the year before, in June, after moving with their son from Zurich to Berlin in April (Einstein had been appointed professor of theoretical physics at ETH, in Zurich, in 1912). Their marriage was no longer tenable. After long being considered an outsider, Einstein was accepted by the scientific community. His renown grew at the speed of light and his obligations increased commensurately, but his own time was not extensible. He worked late into the night. He became more and more frenzied and was constantly traveling. At that time, travel was still very time-consuming and taxing. Sometimes he would be gone for weeks at a time. Under such conditions, how could he maintain a relationship with his wife and children? He found living with

Einstein's sons, Hans Albert (at right) and Eduard, 1919.

Mileva like living in a cemetery. When they were at home alone together, he avoided being in the same room with her.

Mileva's friends noticed that she aged dreadfully during those years. Albert had forgotten her somewhere along the way. As he rose, he left her behind with the role of housewife and mother. Mileva, who had always been a neurotic woman, responded with either vociferous brutality or plain coldness. As for Einstein, his reservoir of emotions dried up. He had invested them all in physics, and now he gradually withdrew into the kingdom of the "uncompromising angels of science," those angels he had always valued more than his wife. Whatever remained of his love for Mileva evaporated. If he felt certain needs, he did not have to wait long to fulfill them. Berlin teemed with brothels, and there was no lack opportunity while he was traveling.

When Mileva left with the children, it was for good. She and Albert never reconciled. His cousin Elsa, who was four years his senior and who had doted on Albert since childhood, was waiting in the wings. Her time had come. She enjoyed all of the attention her cousin, the star, attracted. He offered her the prospect of stepping into a new role, to be a sort of first lady of science. She devised a strategy to introduce her conquest into the upper-crust society she frequented. Above all, she enjoyed glamorous dinners and opening nights at the theater. And she demonstrated true mastery when it came to protecting "her remarkable and delightful adult child" from the vicissitudes of life, as a Russian journalist who had observed the two of them in Berlin later reminisced. She quickly learned to fend off demands of all sorts, so that he could be free to think, while she took care of mundane matters and social relations.

At first Einstein was ill at ease in Berlin. The city seemed decadent and uncultured to him. The Berliners, he grumbled, were all philistines. "When you compare these people with the French and the English, what a difference!" he wrote. "How brutish and primitive they are. Vain, but with no real self-awareness. Civilized (teeth properly brushed, elegant cravats, impeccable suits), but no personal culture (brutish in speech, movements, voice, sensibility)." When Elsa asked Einstein to "be a little accommodating at least" at the rare social events he allowed her to drag him to, his response was, "If you find me so unsavory, find yourself a friend who is more palatable to your feminine taste." He closed one letter to her "with an energetic expletive, your sincerely grungy Albert." He opened the next letter with a "joyful hand-kiss, but from a distance that disinfects, sterilizes, etc." And this time, he signed it "your incorrigible pig."

The pig was now one of the leading physicists of his day, his special theory of relativity having been recognized as revolutionary. But this was far from enough for him—he was overcome by feelings of imperfection. Paradoxical as it may seem, his theory was too theoretical for his liking. Admittedly, it explained the strange processes of light and its observation, but it said nothing about acceleration or terrestrial attraction. In 1915 Einstein developed the general theory of relativity. On March 20, 1916, it was published in the *Annalen der Physik*.

Nine years earlier, while gazing at the roofs of the old city of Bern from his window at the Patent Office, Einstein had an idea that he claimed was "the luckiest [one] of my life."

"For an observer in free fall from the roof of his house, there is no gravitational field—at least not in his immediate proximity." Once again, he shook the foundations of the Newtonian universe. Newton thought of terrestrial attraction—gravity—as a force whereby a great mass attracts other masses. Einstein, on the contrary, believed that such energy was part of the space-time continuum through which cosmic objects travel. The picture was now complete. "Space-time" was born, and with it, the fourth dimension. In this cosmos, matter tells space how it should curve, and space tells matter how it should travel. In 1919, Einstein told his younger son, Eduard, "When a blind beetle crawls along a curved branch, he doesn't notice that it is curved. It was my luck to notice what the beetle didn't notice." Now it was his luck to have a decisive influence on our perception of the cosmos. The Big Bang theory, the expanding universe, the concept of parallel universes—all of these hark back to the general theory of relativity. In his elegant formulas, Einstein even predicted the existence of black holes and phenomena such as quasars. An expedition of British astronomers, led by Arthur Eddington, to observe a solar eclipse would confirm the general theory of relativity. When the telegram announcing this arrived on September 22, 1919, Einstein, who had a tendency to gloat on such occasions, called it "the greatest day of my life."

By that time, he was already married to Elsa. He had been divorced from Mileva in February, and she was granted custody of the children. The German Reich had capitulated the previous year, ending World War I. The emperor abdicated, and a republic was proclaimed. Einstein was enthused by the beginning of this new era.

The war had cost millions of lives, and prominent German intellectuals had played a dubious role in it. It was not only that nearly all physicists had worked for the war machine; lugubrious, nationalistic pamphlets such as the *Appeal to the Cultured World* had been distributed worldwide "against the lies and defamations that our enemies are using in an attempt to besmirch the pure German cause in the hard life-and-death struggle forced upon them." They denied that Germany was responsible for the war and charged the French and British with "allying themselves with the Russians and Serbs and offering the world the shameful spectacle of Mongols and Negroes unleashed against the white race."

The raving nationalists concluded their manifesto by assuring the world that "we shall fight this battle to the end, as a cultured nation to whom the heritage of Goethe, Beethoven, and Kant is as sacred as its hearths and plots of land." Max Planck, Wilhelm Röntgen, Walther Nernst, and Fritz Haber signed it. They had all dedicated themselves, body and soul, to the war machine. This was particularly true of Haber, whose inventions prepared the army for the severe Russian winter. And Nernst performed experiments with tear gas. Einstein, the pacifist, shocked by his colleagues' behavior, refused to sign it. His childlike naïveté—one of the important reasons for his success—and his faith in the inherent goodness of men, remained traits of his character all his life.

Elsa's cardiologist, Georg Nicolai, who also attended the emperor, was a leading pacifist. He proposed to one hundred intellectuals that they sign a response to the *Appeal to the Cultured World*. "No passion can excuse such attitude," it read. "It is unworthy of what the entire world has hitherto understood by the term culture, and it would be a disaster if this were to be the common heritage of educated people." Only four signed the manifesto, including Albert Einstein. In late 1914, he wrote to his friend, Paul Ehrenfest, "This international catastrophe weighs heavily on me as an international individual. Living through this 'great era,' it is hard to believe that we belong to this crazy degenerate species, which claims to possess freedom of will. If only there were an island somewhere for people of good will and prudent character. There I too would be an ardent patriot." So the war greatly pained this man, who loved humanity.

He could hardly sleep and suffered from apocalyptic visions. This was in addition to the superhuman intellectual effort that his work on the general theory of relativity cost him. It was all too much for his body: he collapsed and rapidly lost weight. He became a mere shadow of his former self. Though he was not yet 38 years old, Einstein believed he had cancer and thought he was going to die. He would not leave his apartment and suffered in solitude.

Finally, he was diagnosed with a stomach ulcer. Elsa and her daughters, from a previous marriage, nursed him devotedly. He later became close with one of those daughters and may have been her lover for a brief time. He confided to a friend, "I'll leave it up to you to decide whether I should marry the mother or the daughter." He needed to be taken care of, to be mothered and protected from the pressures of the outside world. It did not much matter to him who filled that need.

And what of his own role, as a father, for example? Einstein, who never eradicated the child from his heart of hearts, sometimes behaved like a good father. He built cable cars for Hans Albert out of matches and string, and explained nature to him.

He increasingly projected his own wishes and hopes onto his sons. Perhaps this was because his own father, whom he loved, had been unable to provide him with the intellectual stimulation he needed and, unlike his uncle Jakob, quickly ceased to be an interesting interlocutor. Einstein especially wanted to mentor his elder son, Hans Albert. This was an ongoing source of friction with Mileva, who was now living in Zurich with the children and feared that Albert's family would gain too much influence over her sons and alienate them from her, leaving her in permanent solitude. In her Zurich apartment, she often fell prey to depression. Mileva's frustration at the way Albert had rid himself of her increased daily. But her husband was persistent: "You can easily leave him with me from time to time, Einstein wrote. "Your relationship with him won't suffer in the slightest, as you'll soon realize. My influence will be confined to intellectual and aesthetic realms." He wrote to his son, asking him to learn a duet for piano and violin so they could play music together. Music, explained Einstein, had always played a major role in his life and had opened many doors for him. And he wanted to tell his son about all the interesting things he had been doing recently.

But Hans Albert was under Mileva's sway. He saw his mother's daily suffering and could not forgive his father. When Albert invited him to go hiking in the mountains, Hans dryly refused in a terse postcard. Then, for many years, he would not answer his father's letters. "I think his opinion of me couldn't possibly be any lower," wrote Einstein to his friend Michele Besso, who was increasingly playing the role of confidant and whom Einstein asked to act as a surrogate father to Hans Albert. But Mileva, ever suspicious, stood in his way. She knew that the friends were in close contact and considered Besso to be Albert's factotum. Despite the distance between them, Einstein increasingly sensed how much his son was like him. He, too, was gradually becoming a "solitary animal," hiding behind a mask of silence and inaccessibility—undoubtedly a consequence of his parents' dramatic divorce. It was his way of protecting himself from dangerous emotions. At school, they called him Steinli, or "little stone."

For a time Einstein even considered bringing his son back to Berlin and taking care of him, giving him lessons. But he knew this would never be compatible with his relentless work schedule. He increasingly took consolation in his violin. Hans Albert would later describe the healing effect of that instrument: "Whenever he felt like he was at the end of his rope, or when he encountered a particularly arduous challenge in his work, he sought refuge in music, and all of his problems would melt away." His problems, yes, but not those of others. Hans Albert and his brother paid the cost of the genius's weakness.

When it suited him, Einstein could be a devoted and interested father, but he had his own concept of paternity. Sometimes one way and sometimes another, he ran hot and cold. All child psychologists know that this type of attitude is the most problematic for children. Fluctuations in the amount of attention paid to them, when children are not old enough to understand, can have destructive effects that go far beyond the realm of the relationship with their parents. Such behavior can also affect the children's ability to sustain lasting relationships, and can even induce significant emotional disturbances. Consistency, say psychologists, is the most important element of a sensible upbringing.

While Einstein's relationship with his elder son was already difficult, his relationship with his younger son, Eduard, could hardly have been more complex. From the start, the boy, who was nicknamed Tete, troubled him deeply. Eduard learned to read at a very young age. He was soon capable of reciting long passages from the works of Goethe and Schiller by heart. His command of language was extraordinary—that alone was enough to concern Einstein, who, as a child, started to speak extremely late. There was something in Eduard that was beyond the genius's control, and a communication block developed between the father and the son. What concerned Einstein was not only Tete's intelligence, but, above all, the behavior of this child who was hypersensitive, nervous, irritable, and vulnerable to illness. The father thought this betrayed a "feminine" and hypochondriacal character. In truth, the child had emotional problems that

Albert Einstein in his office, 1916.

were constantly getting worse. Einstein knew this, and it worried him. Emotional imbalance put him on the defensive, as it always would throughout his life. It stemmed from the repression he constantly applied on the complexity of his own emotional makeup. He just did not want to deal with it. On the other hand, he himself came to the grim conclusion that Eduard had emotional problems, and had no illusions about the boy's future.

He believed his son's chronic illness was a result of scrofula (a disease of the lymphatic glands that Mileva had suffered). When Eduard had been conceived, Einstein had noticed that his wife's lymp nodes were swollen, but did not really pay it much attention. Besides, it was genes that were responsible for all this—Mileva's genes, of course. One day Einstein said with inconceivable coldness, "Who knows if it would not be better if he were to depart before knowing life properly." But he was capable of even worse. Einstein claimed he was "inwardly convinced" that it was "in the public interest do as the Spartans did—"in other words, drop the child off outside the city and abandon him to the natural elements. His attitude had been no less cold with regard to Lieserl, the daughter he never saw. However, at that moment, the genius had been suffering from nervous exhaustion. When the tragedy of his younger son began, ten years later, Einstein remained impassive. His fear of the abysses of the soul had won out.

For the time being, Albert Einstein continued his ineluctable climb to the zenith of his career. During the second decade of the twentieth century, the theory of relativity was all the rage, well beyond the confines of the world of physics. The masses lionized Einstein, revered him as a sage, even though they had not the slightest idea what lay behind that intellectual exterior. "Lights All Askew in the Heavens... Einstein Theory Triumphs" ran the *New York Times* headline, and the president of the honorable Royal Society in London called the confirmation of the theory of relativity "one of the highest achievements of human thought." Furthermore, the theory was utterly in tune with the spirit of the times. That at least partially explains its origin, but also its immense popular effect. Everyone talked about time. It was no longer a finite dimension that was not open to debate. In literature, James Joyce and Marcel Proust were challenging dogma; in philosophy, Henri Bergson introduced the concept of "duration"—the flow of time within the subjective experience. And Friedrich Nietzsche, by describing the "eternal return" of historic cycles, raised history out of the pale of time. In music, the rules of rhythm became parenthetical. In painting, abstraction began to illustrate the new perception in a major way.

Was it mere coincidence that Einstein published his theory of relativity in 1905 and, shortly thereafter,

Pablo Picasso began working on his *Demoiselles d'Avignon,* the abstract painting that seems to abolish all rules of space? Einstein attributed an entirely new role to the observer in the cosmos and destroyed the Newtonian perception of the universe. Picasso abandoned the fixed point of view of the observer and, with it, the central perspective that had been invented by the Renaissance masters.

In 1916, with the general theory of relativity, Einstein brought the central concept of his work to completion. Picasso continued painting his *Demoiselles.* Around 1920, the painter's genius was finally recognized and Einstein's glory was also established. "The world is a curious madhouse," he wrote in September of that year, "at present every coachman and every waiter argues about whether or not the relativity theory is correct." He was a sort of living Copernicus who gave the war-weary Germans —and not them alone—new hope, a "secularized Christmas message," as Albrecht Fölsing said. "He appeared as a personification of Kant's postulate of 'the starry sky above and the moral law within'." Even though the meaning and implications of the theory of relativity were incomprehensible to the masses, Einstein nevertheless became an icon. He had the impression of being an "idol" and hoped "that this would pass, with the help of God." It struck him as "unfair, and even in bad taste" that a few individuals should be singled out for boundless admiration, lending them "superhuman powers of mind and character. This has become my fate, yet there is a grotesque contradiction between the powers and achievements people attribute to me and the reality. Awareness of this curious state of affairs would be unbearable but for one fine consoling thought: it is a welcome symptom in an age that is commonly denounced as materialistic, that it makes heroes of men whose ambitions lie wholly in the spiritual and moral sphere."

Four years before receiving the Nobel Prize, Einstein had already enticed Mileva with the prospect of the award of 120,000 Swedish crowns (17,270 US dollars). That sum, he told her, would ensure their future. Was it then an act of morality when Einstein gave his Nobel Prize award money to his ex-wife, Mileva, who was taking care of Eduard? Was it his guilty conscience speaking, or was it his staunch, albeit belated, recognition of her contribution to the theory of relativity, which he never otherwise mentioned?

He was thoroughly convinced that he would one day receive the Nobel Prize. Doubt was never one of Albert Einstein's prominent traits. Einstein was awarded the prize in 1922 for his developments on light quanta, and not for his theory of relativity, although both papers had been published in 1905. The news came in 1921, when he was traveling to Japan. He loved that country, and it loved him in return. He always praised the Japanese people for their appreciation of art, their intellectual prowess, and their common sense. Their aesthetic sensibility matched his own—simplicity, accuracy, and intellectual grace, with not an ounce of mundane superficiality, and especially, not a trace of the devastation of war found in Germany, and no overt anti-Semitism. Kobe, Kyoto, Tokyo—for Einstein, these cities were a welcome contrast to the hysteria of Berlin, which urban reform had transformed overnight into a city with a population of three million eight hundred inhabitants in 1920: a colossus on the verge of losing its equilibrium.

Unemployment and rampant inflation were the roots of the catastrophe that was gradually taking shape. But the city had also become a cultural Mecca. The likes of Max Reinhardt and Bertolt

Brecht, Walter Gropius and Arnold Schoenberg, Max Beckmann and Otto Dix, all made Berlin the undisputed Western trendsetter of the day— and Jews were largely responsible for this intellectual and artistic flowering of the Weimar Republic. Next to Einstein's theory of relativity were the work of Sigmund Freud and Alfred Adler in the fields of psychoanalysis and psychology, the dodecaphonic music of Arnold Schoenberg, the sexual sciences of Magnus Hirschfeld, the neo-Kantian philosophy of Ernst Cassirer, the expressionist poetry of Brecht and Weill's *Fourpenny Opera*, and the "Neues Theater" (New Theater) of Max Reinhardt. Not to mention countless glamorous revues with acts like the Tiller Girls and Josephine Baker. The city sparkled with wit and eroticism. It was a hotbed whose denizens were blazing new trails in all areas of the arts and sciences.

Einstein, too, was quickly claimed by Berlin, where he was considered one of the city's geniuses, perhaps the most illustrious of all. They were proud of him. Audiences not only flocked to the theater and major expos, but also attended the classes he gave in Auditorium 122 in large numbers. When he played the violin in the New Synagogue on Oranienburger Strasse, it was an event. He had become a figurehead of the Jewish intelligentsia, and he knew it. Einstein was also famous for his sense of humor, as evidenced by this ditty:

> I never thought the Jews were blessed
> Or even very much to view
> But when compared to all the rest
> I'm happy to be one of you

Writer and bon vivant Count Harry Kessler, another important personage in Berlin at the time, painted an impressive picture in his diary of Einstein's attempt to explain the theory of relativity to him. In 1922 Kessler was invited to a dinner party at the Einsteins' apartment. On that occasion, he noted the difference between his hosts and their guests: "This genial, seemingly almost childlike couple brought a certain naïveté to the dinner, which was somewhat overcrowded with too many representatives of big business... The influence of their goodness and simplicity stripped this typically Berlin society of its customary character and imparted to it a practically patriarchal and magical side."

When the meal was over and all of the guests had departed, Count Kessler stayed behind and asked Einstein to explain this theory of relativity that everyone was talking about. "He told me to imagine a glass globe sitting on the table, with a light placed on the top. On the surface of the sphere were flat circles (in two dimensions) with beetles moving across them. A very simple image. When regarded two-dimensionally, the surface of the sphere was unlimited but finite. Consequently, the beetles were moving (two-dimensionally) across a limitless but finite surface. However, if we looked at the shadows of the beetles projected on the table by the light on the top of the globe, the surface that the shadows cast on the tabletop, extending in all directions, was also limitless, like the surfaces of the globe, but it was still finite. In other words, the number of shadow cones or parts of cones cast across an ideally enlarged tabletop always matched the number of beetles on the globe. And since that number was finite, the number of shadows was necessarily finite as well. So what we had there was a representation of a surface that was admittedly limitless, but still finite. Now, instead of two-dimensional shadows of beetles, if we imagined three-dimensional concentric spheres, we could transpose exactly the same representation. The image would then have a limitless but finite space (in three dimensions)... Yet, he said that the scope of his theory did not reside in these movements and representations, but rather in the relativity of matter, space, and time, in proving that none of those three things existed alone, that each was always a condition of the other two."

Thus, in Count Kessler's long-lost diary, we find what is perhaps the most concrete explanation of the theory of relativity, provided by Einstein himself. There is even a monument to this. Architect Erich Mendelsohn built the Einstein Tower, a architectural metaphor for the scientist's work. It is an observatory and one of the most beautiful products of German Expressionism in all of architecture. Mendelsohn said he wanted to reproduce "the mystery surrounding Einstein's universe." At the time, many such bridges were being built between the arts and the sciences. It was the time of Max Beckmann's paintings and of film masterpieces such as *The Cabinet of Dr. Caligari*, *Nosferatu*, and *Dr. Mabuse*, a time when new and different realities were being explored. Einstein's influence was felt everywhere, if only in the form of an intellectual wind blowing through the 1920s. What everyone began to understand at that time was that the universe was different from what they had previously assumed it to be. Reality was not as it seemed. The stars themselves were not where they had been thought to be. This opened up new possibilities for art. There, too, the perception of space and time was transformed, as was the way it was depicted. From architecture and painting to film, contemporary music, and experimental theater, anything was possible.

When he had the time, Einstein took part in the effervescent life of the city. But when he wanted to work, he retreated to his apartment on Haberlandstrasse, in the tranquil "Bavarian quarter" of Berlin. Those rooms, with their professorial aura, formed a "prosperous, petit bourgeois" home, as one visitor described it. The scientist who almost never wore socks felt like an alien in these comfortable surroundings. His doctor, Janos Plesch, said, "His need for independence was so great that he designated a room in his apartment that was his alone, and even the housekeeper was not allowed to enter it without special permission. It was there that he received his friends when he wanted to have a leisurely discussion with them about all sorts of problems. There, too, that he worked in total isolation. It deeply distressed his good wife, Elsa (whom he often referred to as 'my old lady') that she could not take care of him as thoroughly as usual when he retreated there, but that was exactly what he wanted. Dust and disorder were preferable to dependence."

The bohemian in his bourgeois home. Sometimes he just had to get away. He had his fantasies, and Berlin was a metropolis of pleasure. There was no sexual variant that was not available in the city's countless brothels. It is said that Einstein frequented them on occasion. And he had many affairs, sometimes lengthy and sometimes short-lived. For several years, he had ongoing encounters with his secretary, Betty Neumann, the niece of a close friend. Einstein scholar Robert Schulmann even believes that Betty was the only woman he truly loved. The relationship was broken off when Betty's uncle convinced his niece that Einstein was too old for her. He let her go without a back-ward glance. "He was truly not a sentimental man," said Robert Schulmann. "For him, sexuality was a need to be sated."

Toni Mendel, a widow as elegant as she was wealthy, became his "companion" in 1925. Together they went to concerts and the theater and spent the occasional night at Toni's house in the Wannsee quarter. Elsa was consoled with pralines. Also on the list were Estella Katzenellenbogen, who owned several flower shops, and Margarete Lenbach, who vacationed with him in Caputh (Einstein's house in the country). When she showed up, Elsa had to depart in haste, on the pretext of obligations in Berlin. Albert wanted to go sailing alone with Margarete. Sometimes the beauty would also come to Caputh in secret while Elsa spent a few days with a friend or with her daughter. One day Elsa discovered a skimpy bathing suit in a laundry basket. She berated Albert publicly, but he made no concessions. She was hamstrung by her fear of losing Albert, so she took the good along with the bad.

Why this endless string of affairs? Einstein once told a woman friend that the sight of a beautiful young woman saddened him, because it reminded him of the short time we have on this Earth. He was seeking diversion. He literally wanted "to think about something else," in order to then be free to do the thinking that he deemed truly important. He also needed confirmation of his own worth. Einstein was no saint. He loved to roar with laughter in the company of his lady friends, and he had no hang-ups about it. The Einsteins' housekeeper, Hertha Waldow, recalled his disconcerting habit of leaving his bathrobe untied when he left the bathroom. "One day when my cousin came to visit me at Caputh, the professor was in his bathrobe on the patio. He rose to shake her hand. His bathrobe opened, and he was wearing nothing underneath. My cousin blushed. The professor asked her, 'How long have you been married?' 'Ten years,' she replied. He asked her, 'How many children do you have?' 'Three,' she said. 'And you're still blushing?' asked the professor." Elsa, in any event, was constantly suffering new humiliations. She devoted herself entirely to Albert, and it was she who had to lift his morale when he was under attack by his colleagues.

There was strong opposition to Einstein's theories in scientific circles. Physicist Ernst Gehrcke assailed Einstein and accused him of plagiarism, and Nobel Prize winner (in physics) Philipp von Lenard objected that his theories had no general character. A "task force" was formed to combat the theory of relativity. On August 24, 1920, they held a mass meeting at the Berlin Philharmonic Hall—a group of judgmental critics, envious of Einstein's glory. In that somber atmosphere, many frock-coated speakers sounded the charge against the physicist and his new world image, which they described as "un-German." For more than two centuries, people had believed that the cosmos operated like a precision clock, according to Newton's rules, and now this man was destroying that image. He even spoke of it as an "illusion"— what audacity!

Einstein arrived in time for the second lecture and took notes. Several days later, he published a reply in the *Berliner Tageblatt,* entitled "My Reply—About the Antirelativistic Association." The base polemics and arrogance he displayed in that article earned him many enemies—even among his friends. That was not how scientific debate was conducted, even if your name was Albert Einstein. But now he was able to see where the attacks were coming from, since the founder of the Working Party of German Scientists for the Preservation of Pure Science was Paul Weyland, an obscure anti-Semitic journalist and future member of the Nazi SA. He had no scientific background, yet he poisoned objective discourse with his pamphlets against the "Jew's scientific Dadaism." And with a few notable exceptions, the German physicists joined forces with this right-wing extremist and his growing clique.

Einstein prepared to leave the country. He had received death threats and took them quite seriously. No later than June 24, 1922, when the German minister of foreign affairs, Walther Rathenau, was assassinated by two right-wing former officers, Einstein was one of those who believed the rumors that placed him, along with other Jewish celebrities, on a "list of individuals to be eliminated."

The extreme right-wing newspaper *Staatsbürger-Zeitung* wrote, of Einstein and his "co-religionists," "We consider any German who destroys these scoundrels a benefactor of the German people." In the midst of this "golden age" of the 1920s, Einstein withdrew from public life in Berlin. In a state of near panic, he left for Kiel and intended to ask his friend Hermann Anschütz, the inventor of the gyrocompass, for a job in his factory. With Elsa, he went to look at an old house on the banks of the fjord, where he hoped to finally fulfill his dream of owning a sailboat. He wanted to rest after all those years and, especially, to protect himself against the signs of hostility. But he did not. At the last moment, Einstein knew that such silence could quickly become a tomb, and he began a period of what might be termed an intermittent emigration. He was constantly traveling abroad and was practically never to be seen in the German capital. At the same time, this allowed him to publicize his theory, since Germany was not the only country where it was being challenged in those days.

In the twenties, Einstein went to Austria, Czechoslovakia, Norway, Holland, and even England, where he was received coolly, but where he finally won over the scientists at institutions such as the famous Kings College of London. This was thanks to the quality of Einstein's lectures and his persuasiveness. He was more skilled at using public relations tools than any other physicist of his day. He placed flowers at the tomb of Isaac Newton at Westminster Abbey, a gesture that did not go unnoticed. This scientist from an enemy country conquered hearts in France as well. In March 1922, he gave lectures on the theory of relativity and professed his pacifist beliefs. When he visited Verdun, he said, "Every student in Germany, every student in the world, should be brought here, to show them just how monstrous war is." The German embassy in Paris sent a report, stunning in its candor, to the German Ministry of Foreign Affairs. "If Einstein's visit came off with no major hitches and was even satisfactory, it was for two main reasons. For one thing, Einstein is an astounding character whom the intellectual snobbery of the capital could not overlook. And for another, Einstein had been meticulously made 'presentable' for Paris. Even before his arrival, all the papers had emphasized the fact that he had not signed the 'Manifesto of the Ninety-Three,' that, on the contrary, he had signed a counter-manifesto, that he was known to have opposed the German government during the war, and that, finally, he was of Swiss nationality and had only been born in Germany. Be that as it may, it is clear that Mr. Einstein, who had nevertheless to be considered a German, spread the German spirit and German science and gave them new glory."

Einstein was now the undisputed symbol of German pacifism. But he was increasingly making enemies among the nationalists. He repeatedly warned against fascism. And coming events were to prove him right. Yet, when the attempted coup d'état led by Hitler failed in 1923, he again chose to remain in Berlin. The German capital, with its lively culture and scientific climate, was the environment where Einstein would continue to grow.

$$D = \frac{1}{c} \frac{1}{\ell} \frac{d\ell}{dt} = \frac{1}{c} \frac{1}{P} \frac{dP}{dt}$$

$$D^2 = \frac{1}{P^2} \frac{P_0 - P}{P} \sim \frac{1}{P^2} \qquad (1a)$$

$$D^2 = \frac{\kappa \rho}{3} \frac{P_0 - P}{P_0} \sim \frac{1}{3} \kappa \rho \qquad (2a)$$

$$D^2 \sim 10^{-53}$$

$$\rho \sim 10^{-26}$$

$$P \sim 10^8 \, L. \, J.$$

$$t \sim \cdot 10^{10} \, (10^{11}) \, J$$

Einstein's formulas on his blackboard, around 1930.

1925

In late 1925, it seemed that the extreme political situation that prevailed in Germany had once again calmed down. In any event, in those years Einstein did not pay much attention to politics. An entirely different subject occupied his mind as he meditated while sailing on the Brandenburg Lake, where he found that time spent on the water was "incomparably majestic"—something that affected the very heart of his eternal quest to find the secret of space, time, and matter. Slowly but surely, it was becoming clear that the theory of relativity worked on a grand scale, in the universe, but not at all in the microcosm of the atom. The intellectual structure of quantum mechanics was just emerging. When the young physicist Werner Heisenberg, the father of that theory, retreated to the island of Helgoland, in the North Sea, to escape Göttingen during the allergy season, a revolutionary idea struck him: if we want to measure the speed at which an electron travels around the nucleus of an atom, we can never simultaneously determine its location. And, conversely, we can admittedly determine the location of an electron, but in that case it is impossible to measure its speed. In the subatomic world, we must live with statistical probabilities, with "uncertainty," as Heisenberg put it. This had no validity for Einstein. He himself had undoubtedly had revolutionary ideas, but in his heart of hearts, he was still a traditional scientist. He did not want to live with a lack of certainty. He was firmly convinced that "God does not play dice." Einstein had a fierce confrontation on the subject with Danish scientist Niels Bohr, a specialist in quantum physics. After 1925, little by little, Einstein found himself on the margins of modern research. However, as if to forget Heisenberg's "trick," he began devoting his energies to concretely useful objects.

In the summer of 1925, he returned to Kiel to see his friend Anschütz, this time with his son Hans Albert. After returning from some meetings at the League of Nations Commission, the pacifist gave Anschütz advice on how to perfect his gyrocompass, a tool that provided an alternative to the magnetic compass and proved very useful for military applications. The advantage of this "gyroscope" was its advanced rotation system, which enabled it to work even inside the metal hull of an enclosed submarine. The mechanical effect of the rapidly rotating circle made the needle seek to stay parallel to the axis of the Earth.

Einstein does not seem to have had any scruples about improving this military device, and even less so, since he was well compensated for his advice. Once again he displayed that strange talent which enabled him to rid himself of things he found unpleasant—like a dog shaking off water. A year later, the compass was being tested in a torpedo boat of the Reich's navy, and a Dutch company was skillfully used to circumvent the Treaty of Versailles's ban on exporting military articles.

Nor did the Italian, French, and Japanese fleets waste any time in adopting the system. And the contract Einstein had signed with Anschütz allowed him to profit financially from all this.

But in 1939, he stopped receiving his percentage, which in any event did not amount to a fortune. The gyroscope company went bankrupt in 1938. His biographer, Albrecht Fölsing, noted, "Einstein ...

was at least spared any disquieting thoughts on the propriety of earning royalties from a device which guided U-boats and Japanese aircrafts carriers." No one has ever reported that he was angered by the use of his invention by enemy hands, or even that he ever commented on the subject. Einstein, the inventor: a little-known chapter. In Berlin the Nobel Prize winner developed a noiseless refrigerator in partnership with the brilliant young Hungarian physicist Leo Szilard. This was the same Szilard who would later work on the Manhattan Project to build the atomic bomb and who, in 1939, convinced Einstein to support the project by writing a letter to President Roosevelt. Prototypes of the two tinkerers' refrigerator were built, but for various reasons, it was never marketed. In any event, Einstein was unconcerned.

> It can be fun for a great thinker
> With technique now and then to tinker
> The art of invention is my dada
> And egg-laying à deux is even better—*tra la!*

he wrote in a short quatrain, which he then sent to the manager of a research laboratory with whom he wanted to work on developing a new apparatus to aid the deaf. Einstein was fascinated with technical applications, just as he had been when he worked in the Bern Patent Office.

He held talks with industrialists such as the CEO of Osram, which manufactured lightbulbs. During a visit to the latter's chalet in the Swiss Engadine, Einstein suffered a severe cardiovascular problem. He was transferred to Berlin, where he was treated by the fashionable physician Janos Plesch. Einstein's doctor friends warned him about this character, but he enjoyed the company of the charming Hungarian Jew, and sometimes spent weeks at a lodge on Plesch's magnificent estate at Gatow an der Havel, in Brandenburg. But he also encountered him in the salons of the capital. Plesch held men-only gatherings—in addition to Max Reinhardt and Max Slevogt, his guests included the likes of chemist Fritz Haber and the diplomat Count Rantzau—and chamber music concerts at which Einstein played with pianist Artur Schnabel and famed violinist Fritz Kreisler. The doctor was very observant. Later he would write down his impressions: "One of Einstein's major traits is that he never loses his sense of humor in any situation.

He can laugh himself silly over the littlest things. When he hears a joke he has heard before, he doesn't ruin the punch-line, like so many who like to show off their intelligence. He is particularly fond of witticisms and takes a childlike delight in those that he thinks up himself, although he is capable of blurting out the occasional biting remark among friends. And you can't say he's a prude. Like so many thinkers, he does not delight in obscenity, but neither does he shy away from the salacious.

One sure sign that he is totally absorbed in his thoughts: he constantly twirls one of the curls above his forehead around his finger. His eyebrows and his forehead point upward, such that his eye sockets seem enormous, and his high, clear forehead seems to surround them with a luminous frame. At those moments, you sense that you are in the presence of a powerful mind. But when you look more closely, it seems like his entire brain is located in the front of his head. For, to the great astonishment and great annoyance of drawers, painters, and sculptors, the back of Einstein's skull recedes. That is why no artist has managed to do a decent portrait of him. They must all have been embarrassed by that monstrous head with nothing in the back."

In the meantime, the stock market crash in October 1929 had plunged the world into an unprecedented recession. In Germany unemployment rose dramatically.

That same year, Einstein bought a piece of land in Caputh, a short distance from the gates of Berlin, and had a modern wooden house built by architect Konrad Wachsmann, far from the bustle of the city, with its myriad distractions and unending flow of visitors. He did not have a telephone installed there. As often as possible, he would stay in Caputh, thinking, calculating, writing, playing music. The house was a mere five minutes from Lake Templin. He was now finally able to fulfill his dream of being alone on a lake in his own sailboat. Just four years later, his house would be sacked by the Gestapo. Einstein, who had emigrated by that time, would never return to that place he loved so well.

In 1930 the National Socialists won nearly one-fifth of the seats in the Reichstag. There were daily street battles between Communists and Nazis. The final hour of the liberal Weimar Republic was approaching. Hitler's increasingly aggressive propaganda attributed German poverty to decadent democrats and money-hungry Jews. And new attacks on the "Jewish physique" were heard. The fearsome Professor Lenard spewed his venom against "their preeminent representative, the pure-blooded Jew, Albert Einstein." It was becoming dangerous to live in Germany. But Einstein did not see this yet. In December 1930, when he was asked what he thought about Germany's political future and the role of Hitler, he replied that the latter lived off of the poverty of Germany and would be forgotten as soon as the economy turned around. He would not face the probability of a Fascist regime. Einstein was more concerned with his younger son, Eduard, who had been causing him a great deal of worry.

Eduard had enrolled in medical school in Zurich. He wanted to become a psychiatrist. He liked the ideas of Sigmund Freud and had done in-depth research on psychoanalysis and its methods. Albert Einstein did not understand his son's decision. He himself had met Freud in Berlin. Admittedly, he would later admire him as an ally in his battle against the war. But he termed Freud's ideas "doubtful," and his methods nothing short of "deceptive." Eduard, on the contrary, venerated Freud as a demigod. He hung a photo of the Viennese master above his bed.

In his first year of college, having set his sights on a career, Eduard suddenly had a nervous breakdown. He had always been extremely sensitive and vulnerable, which tended to worry his father. The young man became isolated and withdrawn, and stopped attending his classes. Was this due to unrequited love for an older woman, as has been suggested? Einstein wrote to him with the following advice: "Man is like a bicycle. He can only keep his balance if he is moving forward." Work was his suggested panacea. "Even a genius like Schopenhauer was undone by the lack of a profession," he added. Mileva tried talking with her son, but to no avail. Eduard's letters to his father became nothing short of hateful tirades.

Mileva went to Berlin to discuss the situation with her ex-husband. She wanted to take Eduard home and care for him. But she was obliged to give up. In 1932, Eduard was admitted to the Burghölzli psychiatric hospital in Zurich and was diagnosed with schizophrenia. He heard voices and thought they were real. Insulin and electroshock therapy were administered. Albert Einstein would see his son just one more time, in 1933, during a brief trip to Zurich, when he had already provisionally fled to Switzerland.

This man who managed the difficult task of explaining the world could not deal with his son's illness. He could find no rational explanation for this disease. For Einstein, it was purely and simply a nightmare. A mind out of control, an incurable disease—that frightened him. So he wrote the phenomena off to genetics, remarking that there was a tendency toward severe mental problems in his first wife's family. This was surely also a way of abdicating responsibility and obliging Mileva to take care of Eduard, which she did, selflessly, for the rest of her life.

Eduard's niece, Evelyn Einstein, Hans Albert's adoptive daughter, was the family member closest to Eduard in his final years. She took responsibility for him and visited him regularly at Burghölzli. "He had a tiny, dark room on a corridor that was every bit as dark, totally isolated. It was atrocious," she related. "He was calm and amiable. Clearly, they were giving him tranquilizers. Every time I went there, he, the son of Einstein, wanted to talk about science, and to know exactly what was going on in the outside world. The only dictionary he was allowed to use dated from 1920; in other words, it was already more than thirty years old. In the summer, he sometimes

Einstein's last visit to Mileva and Eduard, 1933.

worked in the garden at the clinic. He was an inventive boy, endowed with great intelligence. In all probability, his IQ was higher than his father's, and from that point of view, Eduard was on a par with him. That may have been part of the problem with their relationship."

Once again, Einstein took his mind off things by traveling. In London he was the guest of honor at a benefit dinner for Eastern European Jews, whose fate particularly concerned him. The ballroom at the Savoy Hotel was packed. The cream of British society wanted to see the icon, the "Jewish Saint," as he ironically called himself, and bask in Einstein's magical aura. Baron Rothschild acted as the host for the affair. The master of ceremonies was the most famous English writer of the period, George Bernard Shaw. When he rose to his towering height, with his impressive white beard, there was total silence in the hall. "Ptolemy and Aristotle, Kepler and Copernicus, Galileo and Newton, terrestrial attraction and relativity, modern astrophysics and God knows what else... That is what I am to speak of here. Best to summarize it all in one sentence: Ptolemy created a universe that lasted two thousand years; Newton's universe lasted three hundred years; Einstein has created a universe that you probably want to hear will never end, but I cannot say how long it will last... In any event, he is the greatest of our contemporaries."

As of 1930, the contemporary in question began taking regular trips to the United States with Elsa. Everywhere they went, they were met with a frenetic greeting. From New York, to Chicago, to San Diego and Pasadena, thousands of people gathered to get a glimpse of the pop star of science. Charlie Chaplin invited the couple to Hollywood for the premiere of *City Lights*. Hundreds of thousands of curiosity seekers crowded the sidewalks. When they saw Einstein pull up in Chaplin's limousine, the crowd roared. Chaplin to Einstein: "They cheer for me because everyone understands me, and they cheer for you because no one understands you." Einstein spoke of his travels: "If I am leading this life in my old age, this gypsy life, it is not due to an innate need, but because of the perilous situation in what they call my country." When traveling, he could forget the mounting problems in Germany. And naturally, he kept telling himself that it would be a good thing to go and work in the United States, but then he would dismiss the idea. The Einsteins loved Europe and felt deeply rooted there. Others saw to the move for him. Unbeknownst to him, a colleague, the physicist Abraham Flexner, was making plans for the future of this man he so admired. Einstein had met Flexner in Pasadena. Flexner spoke to him about his plans for a research institute he wanted to set up in Princeton, New Jersey, with the help of some wealthy sponsors. It was to be a small but top-notch institute, equipped to meet the highest requirements. The first disciplines to be included were theoretical physics and mathematics.

On their return to Germany, the Einsteins could see for themselves just how precarious the situation had become. Hindenburg had been reelected at the instigation of Brüning, who was now being forced to resign as chancellor of the Reich. The way was being cleared for the fatal "national concentration" that would result in Hitler's rise to power. The Nazis were gaining the upper hand. When the Einsteins returned from Caputh to Berlin, they learned that a friend of Elsa's, the journalist Antonina Vallentin, had heard a group of young National Socialists denouncing the "dirty Jews," and calling for the death of the vice president of the Berlin police, Bernhard Weiss. The minister of propaganda, Joseph Goebbels, had depicted Weiss as a caricature for the Jewish people, calling him "Isidor." In their morbid imaginations, the young Nazis pictured the scene with relish. They wanted to "chase his naked wife through the streets of Berlin, and set her on fire from the front and from the back." Antonina was horrified. She told Elsa about the episode and urged her to take Albert and leave the country as soon as possible.

"With Albert, that's not so simple," replied Elsa. "He's infatuated with Caputh and doesn't think about anything else. He leads an ideal life there that he wouldn't have elsewhere. He also told me that, for now, no one will get him to leave. He knows no fear." Shortly before, Abraham Flexner had come to visit them at Caputh with a more concrete proposal. His Institute for Advanced Study was taking shape in Princeton. Einstein would have every opportunity there and, naturally, would be the figurehead of the institute. He would spend the winter semester in Princeton, but could return to conduct his research and give courses in Berlin in the summer. So, for the time being, there was no question of emigrating permanently to the United States, but it was still a step in that direction. On July 31, 1932, the National Socialists won 37 percent of the seats in the Reichstag, becoming the majority party in the German parliament.

"Albert is still sailing every day. It's as if he still needs to fill himself, to stuff himself with that pleasure," wrote Elsa on September 29. For her part, she had secretly bid her adieu to Caputh long ago. Then things started happening quickly. One of the last letters Albert Einstein wrote from Germany was addressed to Sigmund Freud. The correspondence between the two visionaries would be published the following year under the title *Why War?*

In December 1932, Einstein was still preparing his courses for the start of the academic year in Berlin. He made no changes to his seminar schedule and scheduled various appointments, as if nothing out of the ordinary were happening. Then Albert and Elsa went to Caputh to ready the house for the winter. It was a sunny day. The lake sparkled through the branches of the bare trees in the garden. The boat had long been in a dry dock at the Plesch storage facility in Gatow. Yet Einstein was not emotional. He calmly said to his wife, "Talk a good look at it, because you'll never see it again." The exodus had begun. They boarded a steamer for Pasadena. One month later, Hitler seized power.

Albert Einstein had no intention of ever setting foot on German soil again. He proclaimed this publicly in America on March 10, 1933, before making a return visit to Europe. Two weeks later, he announced his resignation from the Prussian Academy of Sciences and declared that he was severing all ties with official German institutions. The country had driven out this great mind. In the meantime, the Gestapo had sacked the house in Caputh. Officially, they were looking for arms hidden by the Communists. They found only a

Adventurers and nature lovers:
Einstein and his wife, Elsa, at the Grand Canyon, 1931.

bread knife. Then, early in the summer, it was the apartment on Haberlandstrasse. One evening an SA squad burst onto the scene, to the great surprise of Helen Dukas (Einstein's secretary), Einstein's adoptive daughter Margot, and the housekeeper, who had remained behind in Berlin. Calling out obscenities, over the protests of the women, the looters loaded everything but a few pieces of furniture—porcelain, silver, furnishings, rugs, and paintings—onto a truck. Helen Dukas watched as the mementos that she was supposed to bring with her to the United States also disappeared. In addition, all of the Einsteins' bank accounts were closed. When she learned of this, Elsa urged her husband to use his international contacts to do something about it. But Albert refused to use his influence "for private matters." He retained his spirit of sarcasm. "Our sailboat and our friends stayed behind in Berlin. But Hitler took only the former, which is an insult to the latter."

The Einsteins returned to Europe early that year. They stayed in Belgium and England. In an interview he gave in London, Albert wondered why the civilized world met modern barbarism with passivity. "Doesn't the world see that Hitler's objective is to make war?" On October 3, at the Royal Albert Hall in London, Albert Einstein revealed his goals. A meeting held to support German refugees became his first major forum in his role as activist and prophet of doom. Strictly speaking, he was no longer a pacifist. World War I and its atrocities were still very much on his mind, and he was emphatic that another catastrophe had to be prevented. But above all, it was now a matter of saving civilization. Leading statesmen had to join forces to accomplish this. Hitler had to be defeated, regardless of the cost, passive resistance would no longer suffice to get the job done. Hopes of a moral conversion were a thing of the past; the steamroller of inhumanity was in motion. Einstein knew the Germans, and they knew that their forces could not stop him.

Leaving Southampton, England, the Einsteins boarded the *Westernland*, an American ship, to return to New York. This time, Einstein demanded that "no noise" be made about his arrival. There were to be no cheerleaders and no boisterous crowds. Everything was to be done as discreetly as possible. Einstein, Elsa, Helen Dukas, and Einstein's assistant, Walther Mayer, were taken in a rowboat directly to the Battery in Manhattan, to complete the formalities of entering the country. Then they drove for two straight hours to Princeton, where the new Institute for Advanced Study awaited them. Albert Einstein would henceforth be working in its mathematics department. This was the concrete fulfillment of Abraham Flexner's plan. But what his star scientist did not expect was that, in a certain sense, he would be treated there as a slave. Flexner wanted to prevent Einstein from appearing in public at all costs. The institute was to be protected from the outside world, like a luxurious ivory tower. This did not suit an activist who was increasingly taking his goal to heart. Einstein was obliged to cancel his appearances at benefits. His mail was intercepted. The institute even concealed an invitation to the White House from him. When the recipient learned of this through a circuitous route, he seethed with rage. It was a New York rabbi who made contact for him with Franklin Delano Roosevelt. Einstein complained to the rabbi, in unflattering terms, about Flexner's behavior. The return address he wrote on the letter was "Concentration camp, Princeton." Einstein was given the task of calling attention to the fate of the German Jews by meeting with the president and arranging for media coverage of the event. On January 24, 1934, Elsa and Albert were invited to meet with the Roosevelts and spent the night at the White House.

In any event, the new life the Einsteins led in Princeton had aspects that were not positive. The exile remained an exile. Einstein missed Berlin. At one point, he wrote to his friend Michele Besso that one had to experience America in order to really appreciate Europe. "Of course, the people have fewer prejudices, but most of them are more conventional and uninteresting than they are back home." American women in particular did not appeal to him. He quickly came to that conclusion when the Women Patriot Corporation, an ultraconservative women's group, came out against granting Einstein a visa to enter the United States. They considered him an extremely dangerous leftist agitator. His reaction: "Never yet have I experienced from the fair sex such energetic rejection of all advances; or, if I have, never from so many at once. But are they not quite right, these watchful citizenesses? Why should one open one's doors to a person who devours hard-boiled capitalists with as much appetite and gusto as the Cretan Minotaur in days gone by devoured luscious Greek maidens, and on top of that is low-down enough to reject every sort of war, except the unavoidable war with one's own wife? Therefore give heed to your clever and patriotic womenfolk, and remember that the Capitol of mighty Rome was once saved by the cackling of its faithful geese."

In Princeton, too, even at an advanced age, Einstein would have his lady friends. Of all those who are known, none was an American. Elsa was often homesick for Berlin and a glamorous life that was nonexistent in a small university town. What she missed, as the couple's friend, the biochemist and pharmacologist Leon Watters later related, "was the sympathy and affection of the good old days, and from that perspective, she felt very much alone."

The greatest shadow on Elsa's last years (she died in 1936) was the death of her daughter, Ilse. In May 1934, she received news from Paris that Ilse had an incurable disease and did not have long to live. Einstein let his wife travel to Paris alone. He went with her to the boat in New York, but ended up saying that a few weeks of complete rest would do her a lot of good at her age.

Until 1935 the Einsteins lived in a rental apartment in Princeton. Then they bought a wooden house that looked like it was straight out of an American picture book. It was painted yellow, with a front porch, double-hung windows, and a beautiful garden, like New England in all its splendor. Soon 112 Mercer Street would be as well known as 10 Downing Street or 1600 Pennsylvania Avenue. Yet the man who lived at that address was just an aging, somewhat unkempt professor who spent his time cogitating in his second-story office, furnished with the few pieces of furniture that he had managed to bring from Berlin, with a view of some venerable trees and the graduate college of the university. That atmosphere seemed custom-made for Einstein. He was no longer required to suffer wearing a tuxedo, and at Princeton he enjoyed the almost total freedom of a court jester. He asked the police not to give out his address, even when the requester was insistent. The officers obeyed him to the letter. In his early days at Princeton, Einstein got lost and could not find his way home. He called the police and asked them for directions to Mercer Street. He identified himself, but they refused to help him. They took him for a crackpot or an impostor and told him he could just ask some passersby in the street. That was exactly what he wanted to avoid.

Einstein in his office at Princeton, 1935.

1935

In the fall of 1935, shortly before moving to Mercer Street, Elsa was diagnosed with retinal edema, a complication of severe heart and kidney failure. It was the beginning of the end. She was treated by the best specialists in New York. Obliged to spend most of her time lying down, she became weaker by the day. She watched her "little Albert" moping around the house, depressed. This touched her. "I never would have thought he was so fond of me. It does my heart good," she wrote her friend Antonina.

On the contrary, Einstein's colleague Peter Bergmann recounted that had he worked with his boss at his home during those months and there were constant cries of agony and wailing from the next room, where Elsa lay dying. Bergmann himself found it distressing, but Einstein was so focused on his work that he seemed to notice absolutely nothing. Avoidance remained one of his major ways of coping.

It was perhaps even a question of survival. On December 20, 1936, one month before her sixty-first birthday, Elsa Einstein died. One month later, her widower wrote to his colleague Max Born and mentioned his wife's death only in passing. "I have adjusted extremely well to life here. Here, I'm like a bear in my den ... This bearishness has further increased since the death of my companion, who was better with other people than I am." Later he would tell the young archivist Gillet Griffin that he found solitude "particularly savory." His walks on campus and in the black neighborhoods of the city were also conducted alone. He had made the acquaintance of some African Americans, an assistant cook and a printer, who worked at his institute, and they introduced him to that "society located on the other side of the tracks." Einstein felt a burning interest in the fate of the Negroes, as they were still officially known at the time.

There was still strict racial discrimination in those days, twenty years before Martin Luther King Jr. arrived on the scene. When Einstein went for appointments at the hospital in Princeton, the shortest route took him through the black ghetto. That is how he discovered the neighborhood.

Everyone else took a detour to avoid passing through it, but Einstein used the slightest excuse to explore those streets, which held a certain fascination for him. He felt at ease there, because it seemed to be the only place where he was treated like a normal person. And he felt a curious affinity for the people who lived in the black neighborhood. It was another world, but one that was somehow familiar to him, contrary to the American society in which he lived. "I am no longer part of the world of men here," he complained one day. "I was already too old for this when I arrived. What's more, it was the same in Berlin and in Switzerland. When you're born a loner, a loner you remain." That was the case with Einstein. In the black ghetto, no one bothered him. There, almost everyone was illiterate, so no one had seen his picture in the newspaper. And they never took any pictures either. Everywhere he went, he was the only white. He often stopped to speak with residents on their front stoop or beside a crumbing shanty, to talk about the weather, the latest gossip, and, especially, the situation of the black people, their life, and the discrimination they experienced. He wanted to know, to understand, to feel. Sometimes a colleague's black housekeeper came to pick him up on Mercer Street and take him to the ghetto, where she had introduced him to her relatives and friends. Later he would support singer and activist Paul Robeson and other black leaders in their battle against racism.

He became friends with Robeson and supported his petitions against racial discrimination and lynch-mob justice. He joined in supporting the Progressive Party of Henry Wallace, who demonstrated against civil rights violations and the repression of dissidents. Robeson, an international star, had his passport confiscated and could no longer leave the country. He was under constant FBI surveillance. Einstein hosted his friend several times in Princeton, along with black singer and civil rights activist Marian Anderson. Both had been banned from Princeton for "un-American activities." Einstein nevertheless encouraged them to give a concert there and invited them to stay at his home. By that time, he had long been a problem for the authorities. But Einstein was a philanthropist in an abstract sense. It probably would never have occurred to him to hire a black housekeeper. The "sage of Princeton," as he was now known, shared his home with Elsa's daughter, Margot, and his secretary, Helen Dukas. In 1939 he also brought his beloved sister, Maja, to live with him. Already, he had long been an "institution" of science. But his scientific work was not yet completed. With physicists Banesh Hoffmann and Leopold Infeld, Einstein expanded the theory of general relativity so that it encompassed not only space, time, and gravitation, but also the dynamics of matter.

Working with him, Hoffmann and Infeld found that, even more than in the past, Albert Einstein functioned like an artist, playful and open to everything, with that child's eye to which Henri Matisse also laid claim. Einstein the physicist also operated by intuition and employed concepts such as beauty. He knew that it was easier to understand and describe the laws of nature that way than with logic alone. Having a sense for such things, in addition to a natural talent for mathematics, made all the difference. And at its best, the result is what Matisse called a soothing (visual, in his case) of the mind. For Matisse this meant a well-executed painting, and for Einstein a particularly clear, concise, and therefore beautiful formula. Albrecht Fölsing attributes another source to Einstein's extraordinary way of thinking: "He profoundly

Einstein: a life spent searching the cosmos.

believed, with religious fervor, that simple laws existed, and that these could be discovered. Except for a brief phase during his adolescence, he never had any use for the personified God of the Judeo-Christian tradition. But even in his younger years, he saw God as the guarantor of the laws of nature. Initially this sounded like a playful formulation, but as he grew older the metaphor became a kind of heuristic principle: Einstein would attempt to slip into the role of the creator of the world and its laws."

He actually said to the collaborator of his old age, Banesh Hoffmann, "When I am judging a theory, I ask myself whether, if I were God, I would have arranged the world in such a way." Every morning he awoke with that idea. Einstein would never achieve his true objective of finding the universal formula, the "theory of everything" that, three generations later, scientists around the world are still attempting to find, using ever more costly methods. In Princeton, removed from the scientific community, Einstein worked on the "unified field theory." Its end result was to have been that universal formula, combining all physical forces into as short an equation as possible. But he never did manage to reveal the face of God behind the veil. And neither has anyone else.

In July 1939, Einstein was abruptly wrested from his reflections. Two colleagues, Leo Szilard and Eugene Wigner, came to visit him on Long Island. He had rented a very simple beach cottage in Nassau Point, on Great Peconic Bay, on the eastern shore of the peninsula, from a Dr. Moore, and went sailing every day in the sheltered bay. The physicists were very worried. There were indications that led them to believe that the Nazis were working on an atomic bomb. The previous year, Otto Hahn and Fritz Strassmann had succeeded in splitting uranium nuclei at the Kaiser Wilhelm Institute in Berlin-Dahlem. Lise Meitner provided the theoretical basis and showed that Einstein's formula, $E=mc^2$, "was the key to the enormous release of energy that occurs when nuclei are split." Enrico Fermi and Leo Szilard in New York and Frédéric Joliot-Curie in Paris expanded upon this work and made the decisive discovery: when a uranium nucleus is split by a neutron, two other neutrons are released, resulting in uranium fission. They had discovered the chain reaction capable of infinitely multiplying the destructive power of a bomb. In a fifteen-minute discussion, Szilard and Wigner explained the situation to Einstein. He previously had only a vague knowledge of this field, but he grasped the situation immediately. He was also extremely surprised. He had just predicted in *The New York Times* that the concept of nuclear energy would never find a practical application in his lifetime. What did these two physicists who had come to visit him on this torrid summer day expect of him? They asked him to write a letter to his close friend, the queen of Belgium, with whom he maintained a sporadic but intimate correspondence. The Belgian Congo had uranium deposits that the Americans wanted to get their hands on. They wanted to build the atomic bomb, and they wanted to beat the Nazis to it.

He wrote that letter, not to the queen, but to the Belgian government. Not long afterward, after speaking with a close adviser to the American president, he also wrote a letter to Franklin D. Roosevelt. Einstein asked him to do whatever it took to build an American bomb as quickly as possible, more quickly than the Germans. Because, he wrote in that letter, "A single bomb of this type, carried by boat or exploded in a port, might well destroy the whole port with some of the surrounding territory." The idea that, with such a weapon, Nazi Germany could conquer the civilized world was enough to make any thinking person shiver in horror. Einstein had no trouble imagining the horror of such a war, regardless of which side used the bomb. But just then, he had no choice. He signed the letter. Two months earlier, Hitler and Mussolini had entered into a pact. Europe would become

Fascist, come what may. On September 1, Hitler's troops invaded Poland, signaling the beginning of World War II.

It would be another two years before the start of the biggest research project of all time, the Manhattan Project, which would result in the construction of the American atomic bomb. The best scientists were brought together at the secret Los Alamos Laboratory in New Mexico. Einstein was not one of them. He could only stand by and watch as his Princeton institute was progressively depleted of his colleagues, who left a mysterious forwarding address in Sante Fe, New Mexico.

The authorities were extremely suspicious of Einstein; they considered him a security risk to the enterprise. From the moment he set foot on American soil, the FBI, under the direction of the quasi-paranoid J. Edgar Hoover, never took its eyes off him. Hoover believed that Einstein was a Communist and suspected him of spying for the Soviet Union. Einstein's 1,427-page FBI file is now public record. It contains not only a laundry list of the scientist's activities in the United States— everything from his private life to his pacifist writings—but also of his "prior life" in Germany.

Einstein walking to his beloved sailboat, around 1930.

There are even drawings of his apartment in Berlin, described as a "Communist center," and of his house at Caputh, allegedly a "hideout for envoys from Moscow." All of the organizations he worked with were considered suspect, whether they were Spanish anti-Fascist movements or black civil rights groups. This was considered sufficient motive for the FBI to keep Einstein under almost constant surveillance in the United States and for FBI agents to interrogate his entourage. But they did not dare interrogate Einstein himself. Even now, the FBI still has a sealed file on him, marked TREASON, an offense punishable by death. Such files are not accessible, and, of course, this one cannot be published, even fifty years after the death of the suspect. Yet Einstein was never indicted. So the origin of this very serious charge of treason remains unknown. "Hoover and his men hated Einstein because he was a 'red.' The paranoia of McCarthyism may have magnified all that, but there was no question of his being a traitor," says Einstein scholar Fred Jerome. "The mystery may never be solved, because publication of the file would be an embarrassment to the FBI. After all, it would be tantamount to accusing Jesus Christ of treason."

Einstein the "traitor" became an American citizen, although he never gave up his Swiss citizenship. But this did not stop the U.S. Navy from asking him for his advice on the use of highly explosive substances. His task was to research the best way of exploding torpedoes. Once again, he gladly embarked on a tinkering job that paid him only twenty-five dollars a day. He joked that he was "the only one in the navy who didn't have to cut his hair." That being said, these small jobs for the navy were no substitute for participation in the historic Manhattan Project. Although he never said so, Einstein was hurt by the fact that he was not asked to help. But life went on on his "island of destiny," as he called Princeton, "where the mingled voices of human combat barely reach me." He remained a lone wolf in his solitude. Robert Oppenheimer, who would soon become known as the "father of the atomic bomb" and would take over as director of the Institute for Advanced Study, saw Einstein almost daily in his office at Fine Hall, as he searched for the universal formula, covering the big blackboard with formulas and calculations.

"Einstein was the nicest man I've ever known," Oppenheimer later recalled. "I got the feeling that

Evelyn Einstein in Berkeley, California, 1953.

he was very lonely. Many great men are loners. But in his case, although he was a faithful friend, it seemed to me that deep human emotions never played a central role in his life."

But Einstein was always looking for love. During these years, he would mostly find it while traveling. It is said that he had an intimate relationship with a young ballet dancer in New York. This is still a subject of speculation. Some even say that he had a child—a daughter—with her. What's more, according to rumor, that daughter was Evelyn Einstein, the adoptive daughter of his son, Hans Albert. She is still living today, in poverty, near San Francisco. Evelyn, who looks a lot like Einstein and who has a remarkably high IQ, has always suspected that

Albert Einstein might be more than her adoptive grandfather. "Einstein may have more or less gently coerced my father, Hans Albert, to adopt me, in order to be at peace with himself," Evelyn says. "He may have had a guilty conscience because he never took care of his first daughter, Lieserl." And she adds, "All this seems so absurd. But who could refuse a request from Albert Einstein?" One day, the principal of the school that Evelyn attended in Switzerland spoke to Frieda, Hans Albert's wife, about the rumors. She apparently replied, "What do you mean, rumors? It's true!" But that proves nothing. We may never know the truth of the matter.

"Captain Einstein" at Princeton, 1945.

1945

In March 1945, some the physicists who were about to complete their work on the atomic bomb began having qualms. What would be done with their diabolical engine? Germany was close to defeat, and there was no more danger from that quarter. The miracle weapon would never see the light of day on German soil. In that case, what would be done with the American atomic weapon? And what would happen after the war? This genie could never be put back in its bottle. In all likelihood Einstein had not given the matter much thought; that type of conundrum was not his affair. He would not become involved until later. It was Leo Szilard who was the most worried by all this. He wanted to make the president aware of the historic risks this weapon represented. He visited Einstein and once again asked him to write to Roosevelt. After all, the president had taken Einstein's advice before. The letter was written and sent to the president, marked PERSONAL. It read, in part:

"The terms of secrecy under which Dr. Szilard is working at present do not permit him to give me information about his work; however, I understand that he now is greatly concerned about the lack of adequate contact between scientists who are doing this work and those members of your Cabinet who are responsible for formulating policy. In the circumstances I consider it my duty to give Dr. Szilard this introduction, and I wish to express the hope that you will be able to give his presentation of the case your personal attention.

Very truly yours,

Albert Einstein"

No explicit warning about the consequences of the bomb, no particular commitment. Nothing more than the bare essentials. In any event, Roosevelt would never read those lines. He died on April 12. Einstein's letter was found on the president's desk, still sealed. It was forwarded to President Truman, who gave it to his designated secretary of state, James F. Byrnes. A debate was begun between scientists and political leaders in an Interim Committee. The scientists could see "no acceptable alternative to direct military use" of the bomb. Clearly, the clock could not be turned back, and events took their inevitable course. Einstein spent the summer at Saranac Lake, in the Adirondack Mountains, near New York—an ideal spot for sailing. But he worked, too, and Helen Dukas had made the trip with him. Early in the afternoon of August 6, she was listening to the radio

A caricature of Einstein as a bomb.

as Einstein napped and heard the news brief. The Americans had dropped a new type of bomb on the Japanese city of Hiroshima. When Einstein awoke, asking for tea, Helen broke the news. His reaction was even more terse than the news bulletin, "*Oh Weh*. And that's that!" Three days later, a plutonium bomb was dropped on Nagasaki.

On August 12, He told *The New York Times*, "I was in no way involved in the development of the atomic bomb." That was an accurate statement. But questions remain: should he have written the letter to Roosevelt in 1939? When this fact was made public, Einstein immediately went on the defensive. He said he had written it only because he was afraid the Germans were developing their own bomb. Then he tried rationalizing in order to reassure himself—another form of repression—and made this absurd statement, "I do not believe that civilization will be wiped out in a war fought with the atomic bomb. Perhaps two-thirds of the people of the Earth might be killed, but enough men capable of thinking and enough books would be left to start again, and civilization could be restored." And yet, in the years prior to his death, nothing preoccupied him more than the concern of preserving humanity from a nuclear holocaust. That concern gnawed at him and destroyed his health.

His heart was weak and he was plagued with stomach, intestinal, and liver problems, but refused almost all medical attention. Only in an emergency did he place himself in the hands of those "charlatans, most of whom have no accurate knowledge." Most often, he would be admitted to the hospital at the very last moment and, with stoic calm, undergo surgery. His decades of neglecting "the old machine," as he called the body, began to take their toll. But some of his problems were clearly psychosomatic. Even for Einstein, repression had its limits. He had great misgivings about the use of the most horrific weapon ever known by mankind on Hiroshima and, several days later, Nagasaki. The awareness that this weapon was probably here to stay further magnified those feelings. Later his colleagues would recount that he deeply regretted the role he had played and having written the letter to Roosevelt. When Leo Szilard, the instigator of that letter, arrived in Princeton shortly after the bomb fell, he found Einstein meditating in his office. His desk was littered with papers, blackened with formulas for the unified field theory. The papers were interspersed with pipe ash, shreds of tobacco, and a mug half filled with oatmeal. For a long time, Einstein just sat there, twirling a lock of hair around his finger and not saying a word, barely looking at Szilard. Then he said, "I think the ancient Chinese were right. It's impossible to know all of the consequences of one's actions. That's why the sages settled for contemplation." If only he had not left his ivory tower. But the "sage of Princeton" refused to see that the primary source of his dilemma was his discovery, the formula that was the product of his contemplation. It was his formula that had provided the very basis for the bomb. "Why did you take part in producing the atomic bomb?" asked the chief editor of Japan's largest newspaper, *Kaizo*. He answered, "I was well aware of the dreadful danger that the success of that undertaking would represent for humanity. But the probability that the Germans would work on the same project and possibly succeed forced me to do so. I had no other choice, even though I have always been a firm believer in pacifism. To my mind, to kill in war is not a whit better than to commit ordinary murder." Once again, we see the tragic contradictions of his character and his life. When Antonina Vallentin, that astute observer of the Berlin of her day, visited Einstein in Princeton in 1948, she immediately noticed the state he was in. "The most heartrending change was his eyes," she said. "They were surrounded by dark circles, as if burnt, spreading in purple rings and descending to his cheeks. His eyes had sunken into their deep orbits. But nothing could dim that blazing gaze, that dark and inextinguishable fire. That livid face was clearly being consumed from the inside out." She discerned the tragedy within him, even though he had not lost his sense of humor. "But his laughter was brief, as if shriveled. It was no longer a full-throated laugh, but rather a laugh of the lips, the remnant of a laugh."

Since the end of the war, Einstein had been increasingly active in the call for a world government that could impose arms controls and raise an international peace force. Along with Thomas Mann and some leading Americans, he signed a declaration that stated, "We must aim at a Federal constitution of the world, a working worldwide legal order, if we hope to prevent atomic war." The United Nations Charter, signed by fifty-one countries on June 26, 1945, was insufficient, he believed, and would prove to be a "tragic illusion."

Einstein stated, in a speech in New York on December 10, "The war is won—but the peace is not." That seems to have been the motto for the last ten years of his life. Like a watchful guardian, he observed the mad arms race and the start of the Cold War, the constant menacing posturing of the great powers. He expected the worst, and slowly but surely lost the faith in humanity that had been so deeply rooted in him. "If all efforts are in vain and mankind ends in self-destruction, the universe will shed not a single tear over it."

In 1946, the Emergency Committee of Atomic Scientists was founded, with Einstein as its chairman. He publicly called for the great powers to work together in the arena of nuclear weapons rather than working against one another. That, he said, was the only way to avoid a catastrophe. The bomb in enemy hands? Unthinkable! Such ideas were considered totally un-American and once again focused suspicion on Einstein. Would he take advantage of his relations with the atomic scientists to disclose their secrets to the other great power? The authorities were once more in a state of panic. The FBI's subsequent treatment of Einstein became nothing short of a witchhunt. Hoover wanted to strip him of his citizenship and deport him from the country. In the meantime, crusading Communist hunter Joseph McCarthy arrived on the scene. For five years, he poisoned the atmosphere in America. The trials that Senator McCarthy held all around the country were termed "committees"; Einstein wrote to a teacher who had been subpoenaed to testify before one of them, "Every intellectual called before a Congressional investigating committee should refuse to testify and must be prepared for jail and economic ruin, in short for the sacrifice of his personal welfare in the interest of the cultural welfare for his country. If enough individuals are prepared to take this difficult path, they will succeed. Otherwise, the intellectuals of this country deserve nothing better than the slavery to which it seeks to subject them." And he called for civil disobedience. "The only path open to us is to refuse to collaborate, in the spirit of Gandhi." Even the country's great newspapers sided against the physicist. The situation was turning ugly. But Einstein, undaunted, continued his battle against the nuclear arms race. Then things started happening quickly. The president ordered work to commence on a hydrogen bomb. It would have infinitely more destructive force than the previous generation of nuclear weapons. Einstein's Princeton colleagues were already at work on the principle. Robert Oppenheimer assembled a team of his most experienced colleagues, from Enrico Fermi to Edward Teller. Einstein knew what was going on in the conference room below his office, but he did not speak about it with his colleagues. He had long been in isolation. But on February 12, 1950, he addressed the American nation, using the new medium of television for the first time, and was very explicit: "The H-bomb appears on the public horizon as a probably attainable goal. Successful, radioactive poisoning of the atmosphere and, hence, annihilation of all life on earth will have been brought within the range of what is technically possible. The weird aspect of this development lies in its apparently inexorable character. Every step appears as the inevitable consequence of the one that went before. And at the end, looming even clearer, lies general annihilation."

He was also a harsh critic of the intent to build that weapon, which the president had just expressed

Einstein with Margarita Konenkova, his mistress during the years 1935–1945.

Herzlichen Gruss
A. Einstein

publicly, greeted with widespread patriotic fervor. Once again, Einstein's words were interpreted as highly anti-American. If the FBI and the McCarthy hearings had found out that, until 1945—precisely the time when the first bomb was developed—he had been involved in an affair with a beautiful, blonde Russian, Margarita Konenkova, they would have had him cold. Regardless of the popularity of the "sage of Princeton," that affair would have been the straw that broke the camel's back. The cosmopolitan Russian had met Einstein when her husband, sculptor Sergei Konenkov, was creating a bust of the scientist. The attraction was immediate. Einstein liked Margarita because she was intelligent, and her urbanity reminded him of his lady friends in Berlin. She was also quite the eccentric. When she went to visit him, she always brought her pet rats with her.

Konenkova was apparently a Russian agent. There is no concrete proof of this, but it is entirely plausible. What secrets could Einstein have revealed to her? He did not have access to any military secrets. It is barely conceivable that he could have speculated about the contributions the various physicists had made to the Manhattan

Project. When they were together, Albert and his lover surely had much more private matters to discuss. They called one another "Almar," a combined contraction of their first names, and also used that name for their love nest, the house on Mercer Street. Their encounters took place on weekends, when Helen Dukas was away. "But everything here reminds me of you. Almar's blanket, the dictionaries, the wonderful pipe that we thought was missing, and all the other little things in my cell, but also our lonely nest," he wrote to her in Moscow when she returned to live there in 1945. Had she accomplished her mission? In any event, Margarita Konenkova's role remains a mystery. Did Einstein have more information than even those close to him realized? Did he disclose it to her? His FBI file has never been made public in its entirety. Several pages are missing, and long passages have been censored. When asked, the FBI responds that this is due to the TREASON label it once bore. American law prohibits publication of such documents, even fifty years after the death of the subject.

Margarita Konenkova would not be the last woman in Einstein's life. Johanna Fantova succeeded her and set Einstein's regimen for the years preceding his death. He knew Johanna, a widow twenty-two years his junior, from his Berlin days. In the German capital, she had put his library in order and was a daily visitor to the apartment on Haberlandstrasse. They had shared memories— Johanna had been married to the son of the legendary Prague hostess Berta Fanta. Now, increasingly solitary in Princeton, Hanne, as Einstein called Johanna, took care of him. They sailed together on Carnegie Lake and went to movies and concerts. Johanna Fantova was even allowed to cut his famous mane. They spoke on the phone almost every evening. Johanna meticulously noted down every word uttered by her "elephant" (her nickname for him), composing a sort of journal, now an invaluable source of information about Albert's state of mind and his physical decline. "He no longer plays the violin because playing it is too strenuous, but he still plays the piano every day—it's much easier to improvise on it," she wrote in the introduction to her notes, which were not discovered until 2004, in her personal file. "In the evening and often late into the night, he would read to his sister and me. He often interspersed these 'readings,' which were most often from the works of Freud,

Schopenhauer, and Russell, with his own critical comments. Einstein's day began late in the morning. After taking a brief, disparaging look at *The New York Times*, he would go to the Institute every day, accompanied by his old friend, logician Kurt Gödel." Gödel, a famous mathematician who arrived in Princeton in 1940, after fleeing Austria under risky conditions, was one of Einstein's closest associates and probably his closest friend in the ensuing years.

Einstein often met with him and physicist Wolfgang Pauli at his home on Mercer Street to discuss the philosophical roots of science. Bertrand Russell joined them in 1943. Russell recalls in his autobiography, "Although all three of us were Jews, exiles who thought of ourselves as cosmopolitan, we all had a strong inclination for metaphysics, and try as we might, we could never find any common premises for our reasoning." Of course, Einstein was deeply rooted in German culture and language, but his strong aversion to his native country continually increased. He totally dissociated himself from it. Since 1933, his closest—and strongest—tie was his solidarity with his "Jewish brothers," his "tribe." And this attitude was undoubtedly what shaped his position on German society and state. Over the years, asserted physicist and psychologist Johannes Wickert, experiences with Jewish persecution exerted a decisive and ever increasing influence on Einstein and his actions, "as a crystal can takes shape through the accumulation of strata around a crystallization point." One of those points, and it arose more and more often, was his vision for the state of Israel. In his essay "The World as I See It," Einstein wrote, "Judaism seems to me to be concerned almost exclusively with the moral attitude in life and to life." Yet he told his brethren, "Do not gird at fate, but rather look on these events as a reason for remaining true to the cause of the Jewish commonwealth." He believed that bringing the Jews of the Diaspora to their ancient homeland, Palestine, was a "great and noble mission," and he worked energetically toward that goal. On May 14, 1948, the date of Israel's declaration of statehood, Einstein felt a profound satisfaction—although he foresaw that the coexistence of Jews and Arabs, whom he referred to as "our brothers the Arabs," would pose inextricable problems. He felt that if they engaged in armed conflict, the dignity of both peoples would suffer. He offered many detailed proposals for preventing a fratricidal war.

In 1952, a few days after the death of Israel's first president, Chaim Weizmann, Einstein received a request from Prime Minister David Ben-Gurion, who wanted him to become the next president of Israel. He responded to that request politely but firmly: "All my life I have dealt with objective matters, hence I lack both the natural aptitude and the experience to deal properly with people and to exercise official functions. For these reasons alone I would be unsuited to fulfill the duties of that high office, even if advancing age was not making increasing demands on my strength." His visitors during that period had rarely seen Einstein so excited. He smoked one pipe after another as he paced up and down the stairs, murmuring, "This is awkward." He wrote to painter Josef Scharl, who had painted a more perceptive portrait of Einstein than any other artist and who had become a close friend, "I was very touched by the proposal of my Israeli brothers. But I immediately refused it with sincere regret. I know that more than one rebel has become a stuffed shirt, but I can't do it."

So Einstein remained in his "three-woman household," as he described it. His secretary, Helen Dukas, found Johanna Fantova a nuisance. Helen thought of Einstein as her property, which she had to protect at all costs. At one point, she even went so far as to check the private mail addressed to her lord and master, to ascertain whether it would upset him. Yet, when it came to Johanna Fantova, she took the bad with the good. She could see that Einstein was enamored with Johanna. She knew how he was when he was in that state and that he would not listen to her. In 1947, Einstein gave Johanna a fountain pen for Christmas and sent her this unambiguous poem:

> This gift is not like the long, firm, thick beam
> That to Freud means virility when seen in a dream.
> But when writing in the day's bright light
> Its sole purpose is to ease your plight
> Whether imagined or factual
> Its willingness is always actual.
>> For my dear Hanne, her A.E.,
>> Christmas 1947

And on another occasion:

> The pencil is, in some respects
> A symbol of the masculine sex

This should not make Johanna bashful
Since she knows how to wield it well

Clearly, no one was closer to Albert Einstein in his last years. With Johanna, he could truly be himself. Complex thoughts became secondary, while daily life, however ordinary, took priority for brief moments. On November 4, 1953, Einstein spoke of a vision he had in a dream and Johanna Fantova wrote it down. "Last night, I slept poorly and had a very strange dream. I saw my sister's dress, draped over a chair. I tried to fold it, but was unsuccessful, whereupon the dress suddenly disappeared. In place of the dress, which I could no longer find, a friend of mine appeared sitting in the chair. Then I read a book on the interpretation of dreams. Its author scorns Freud, while still giving credence to him." And on November 5, he continued, "Prompted by my dream, today I read passages from Freud's *Totem and Taboo* to my sister. What a strange, tenuous concept is the Oedipus complex, a son's jealousy of his father. It's unreal, this hostility toward the father. Do women have Oedipus complexes? This all seems quite incredible to me. The idea that repressed conflicts are expressed in dreams is not so absurd, but it is dubious. And it is dubious that our actions can be traced back to origins of which we are not aware. ... Freud was very intelligent, but much of his theory is nonsense, and therefore I am opposed to you undergoing analysis." His judgment was still keen, and he was more opinionated than ever.

Nor did Einstein's taste for intellectual experimentation desert him until the end. Formulas remained his elixir of life, and increasingly became a sort of separate world into which he could retreat. On July 30, 1954, he wrote, "After much useless effort, I'm making some progress in my work. If the results fall short of my expectations, I still derive consolation from the fact that confronting problems makes you independent of the human sphere, and that is an inestimable grace." But his health problems were mounting and interfering with that state of grace. On July 30, he told Johanna Fantova, "Nothing brilliant to say about myself today, expect that my old liver is acting up again, and giving me a good deal of pain and nausea. But I'm used to it and am not concerned by it." And two weeks later, "Another relapse. It was awful. I'm not yet ready to give up the ghost, but I am severely diminished and have the feeling that I won't be around much longer and that my brain is very old..."

Shortly thereafter, he was diagnosed with severe hemolytic anemia.

Einstein with Johanna Fantova, his last lover.

1955

In early 1955, Einstein overcame his anemia. But he was obsessed with thoughts of death. On February 5, he wrote, "I perceive death like an old debt that one eventually pays. Yet instinctively one does everything possible to postpone fulfilling this final settlement. Such is the game that nature plays with us. We may ourselves smile that we are that way, but we cannot free ourselves of the instinctive reaction to which we are all subject."

Einstein abandoned himself to the harmony of natural law, the metaphor he used so often in place of the term "God." And he bequeathed to the generations of physicists who would follow him what Einstein scholar Frank Steiner summarized in these words: "Physic and metaphysics have a common root that we may call, along with Einstein, cosmic religiosity. In other words, physics cannot get along without metaphysics."

Einstein must have been very gratified to have found an intellectual partner in Bertrand Russell. Of all the modern philosophers, he was the one Einstein esteemed the most. He felt that Russell confirmed thoughts—not only his theories of physics, but his whole worldview, his deep religiosity, which was the basis for his humanitarian commitment. "To sense that behind anything that can be experienced there is a something that our mind cannot grasp and whose beauty and sublimity reaches us only indirectly and as a feeble reflection, this is religiosity. In this sense, I am religious. To me it suffices to wonder at these secrets and to attempt humbly to grasp with my mind a mere image of the lofty structure of all that there is." He wrote these lines, a sort of profession of faith, in 1930.

On April 11, 1955, in his house, which he practically never left during his final years, Einstein signed an appeal against the arms race. He had written it with his friend, philosopher Bertrand Russell. That afternoon he received Abba Eban, the Israeli ambassador, to discuss the security of Israel in a hostile world. They also spoke of their plans for a radio address on the occasion of the country's impending seventh anniversary. Einstein was weak and constantly nauseous. Two days later, he collapsed in his bathroom. He knew exactly what was happening. It was an aneurysm in his abdominal aorta, diagnosed seven years earlier. But the idea of surgery seemed absurd to him. He did not want to go to the hospital; he wanted to remain at home. He could feel death approaching. "I would like to go when I want to. It is tasteless to prolong life artificially." Helen Dukas remained by his side, day and night, giving him ice cubes and mineral water to keep him from becoming dehydrated. When his doctor told the secretary that she should not assume this responsibility alone, that it was too much for her, she finally allowed him to be transferred to Princeton Hospital. A surgeon was to be brought in from New York to operate on the aneurysm. Einstein refused, despite the horrible pain he was in. Hans Albert arrived from California and attempted to convince his father to undergo the operation, but in vain. During the night of April 17, at around 1:15 a.m., a nurse went into his room, noticed that he was breathing irregularly, and raised his head slightly. Einstein whispered a few words to her in German, which she did not understand, drew two deep breaths, and died. In accordance with the will he had written in 1950, he was cremated. His ashes were scattered on the banks of a bend in the Delaware River, where the willow branches touched the water. Albert Einstein was once more at one with the cosmos whence he had come to unveil its great secret. Shortly before his death, he wrote, "for we physicists believe the separation between past, present, and future is only an illusion, although a convincing one."

Before he was cremated, an autopsy was done on Einstein's body. One of the pathologists who performed the autopsy, Dr. Thomas Harvey, removed the physicist's brain and examined it. Later he sent samples of it to various laboratories. Today research is still being done on its structural characteristics. But Albert Einstein took his secret—the mystery of his mind—with him. All efforts to find a conclusive explanation for his genius have, so far, been in vain. As have the attempts of a new generation of physicists to find a "universal formula."

A photograph that traveled around the world, 1951.

Bibliography

Brian, Denis, *Einstein: A Life*. New York: John Wiley and Sons, 1996.

Calaprice, Alice (ed), *The Expanded Quotable Einstein*. Princeton: Princeton University Press, 2000.

Dukas, Helen and Banesh Hoffmann, *Albert Einstein, The Human Side*. Princeton: Princeton University Press, 1979.

Einstein, Albert, *Ideas and Opinion*. New York: Random House, 1954.

————, *The Meaning of Relativity*. Princeton: Princeton University Press, 1953.

————, *The World as I See It*. New York: Kensington, 2000.

Einstein, Albert and Mileva Maric', *Am Sonntag küss'ich Dich mündlich*. Munich: Piper Verlag, 1994.

Flückiger, Max, *Albert Einstein in Bern*. Bern: Paul Haupt, 1972.

Fölsing, Albrecht, *Albert Einstein: Eine Biographie*. Frankfurt: Suhrkamp Verlag, 1993. English translation: *Albert Einstein*. Translated by Ewald Osers. New York: Penguin Books, 1997.

Hawking, Stephen, Kip Thorne, Igor Novikov, Timothy Ferris, and Alan Lightman, *The Future of Spacetime*. New York: W. W. Norton, 2002.

Highfield, Roger and Paul Carter, *The Private Lives of Albert Einstein*. London: Faber and Faber, 1993.

Kaku, Michio, *Einstein's Cosmos*. New York: Norton, 2003.

Meschkowski, Herbert, *Von Humboldt bis Einstein*. Munich: Piper Verlag, 1989.

Michelmore, Peter, *Einstein: Profile of the Man*. New York: Dodd Mead and Company, 1962.

Plesch, Janos, *Janos: The Story of a Doctor*. Munich: Paul List Verlag, 1949.

Schulmann, Robert (ed), *The Collected Papers of Albert Einstein*, vol. 8. Princeton: Princeton University Press, 1998.

Seelig, Carl, *Albert Einstein*. London: Staples Press, 1956.

Stachel, John (ed), *The Collected Papers of Albert Einstein*, vol. 1 and 2. Princeton: Princeton University Press, 1989.

Steiner, Frank (ed), *Albert Einstein, Genie, Visionär une Legende.* Berlin: Springer Verlag, 2005.

Vallentin, Antonia, *Das Drama Albert Einsteins. Eine Biographie.* Stuttgart: Günther Verlag, 1955.

Weinberg, Steven, *Dreams of a Final Theory.* New York: Pantheon Books, 1992.

Zackheim, Michelle, *Einstein's Daughter: The Search for Lieserl.* New York: Riverhead Books, 1999.

Photo credits

Acknowledgments

The author would especially like to thank:
Evelyn Einstein, Paul Einstein, Prof. Francis Everitt, Gillet Griffin,
Stephen Hawking, Fred Jerome, Prof. Michio Kaku, Prof. Robert
Schulmann, Prof. Frank Steiner, Prof. Brian Greene, Dr. Peter Plesch,
Prof. Steven Weinberg, and Dr. Michelle Zackheim, as well as
Christiane von Boehm and Cristina Trebbi.

The publisher wishes to thank Charles E. Greene and Anna Lee Paul
(Princeton University), Barbara Wolff and Chaya Becker (Einstein
Archives, Jewish National & University Library, Hebrew University
of Jerusalem), Françoise Carminati and Julie Papini (Corbis),
Miriam Intrator (Leo Baeck Institute), Lisa Nugent (Lotte Jacobi
Collection, University of New Hampshire), and Do You Graphic.